MAKING
GOD
FAMOUS

Mal Fletcher

Next W@ve International

Published by Next W@ve International
Visit our website at www.nextwaveinternational.com

ISBN 0-9579020-0-X

1. Christian witness 2. Leadership 3. Young Adult

Unless otherwise stated, Scripture quotations are from the
New International Version of the Bible, copyright 1973, 1978,
1984 by International Bible Society.

Printed and bound in Denmark

Cover Art: Markus Lindell
Main Cover Photographs: Hanna Lindell, Tina Kornbek Meyer

Next W@ve International
Drejervej 11-21, 2400-Copenhagen NV, Denmark
Phone: +45-3531-0097, Fax: +45-3531-0096,
E-mail: nxtwave@csi.com and
255 Old South Rd., Reynella S.A., 5161, Australia
Phone: +61-8-83222888, Fax: +61-8-83228101,
E-mail: garyr@southside.org.au
www.godfamous.com

What major Christian leaders say about Mal Fletcher:

'There are some who merely watch things happen, as the saying goes, and some who make things happen; the observers and the activists. But every now and then you come across a man with the unique ability to do both; he who both sees with a prophet's eye what is going on in a world and has the giftings to affect it with power. Mal Fletcher is one of these men. He is a thinker, an artist, and above all a man who loves God and loves people.'

Winkie Pratney, Author and Evangelist

'Today, we are seeing the emergence of powerful new ideas that are permeating our society. The combination of new ideas and advanced technology sometimes makes the church seem stale, stuffy and irrelevant. One man I know who is addressing the issues, and has insight into what the church needs to become, is my friend Mal Fletcher. He has been a special blessing to myself in this area, giving new insight to me and the body of Christ in South Africa.'

Rev. Ray McCauley, Senior Pastor,
Rhema Church, South Africa.

'Today, there are many people trying to make themselves famous, seeking fame and fortune. Mal Fletcher, however, has proven himself a faithful man of God whose life truly seeks to make GOD famous. He has a powerful anointing to communicate the gospel and his life inspires many, including Mark and me, as he follows the call of God to change the face of Europe. Not only will this book bless and inspire you; it will challenge you to do everything you can to make God famous today!'

Darlene Zschech, Hillsongs Music.

'Mal Fletcher is an Aussie legend. Rarely has someone left our shores with so little and accomplished so much. I believe Mal is *an end-time leader with an amazing anointing on his life. His integrity and his passion so inspire me. Mal's my hero!'*

Pastor Jack Hanes, President, First Priority (AOG World Missions), Australia.

'Mal Fletcher is a key communicator in today's culture. He carries the unique blend of creative and provocative thought with a solid and biblical foundation. His is not just a man of words but also a man of action. The fruit of his ministry can be seen right across Europe.'

Pastor Stuart Bell, Leader, Ground Level Network of Churches, UK.

'As a friend and colleague of Mal Fletcher, I have always found his written works to be both stimulating and faith building. I consider reading a Mal Fletcher book a must. It will always leave you feeling equipped and ready for the leadership challenge.'

Pastor Danny Guglielmucci, Senior Pastor, Southside Christian Church, Australia.

'Mal Fletcher has the unique ability to discern the needs in today's international Western culture and to articulate, in a powerful, relevant way, the biblical solutions to those needs. He is being used by God to help shape the emerging leaders in today's church, especially throughout Western Europe. Mal is a man with a message that needs to be heard.'

Bayless Conley, Senior Pastor, Cottonwood Christian Centre, Los Alamitos, USA

'Mal has committed his life to making God famous, and his passion for this purpose has influenced thousands of young adults all over the earth to go out and do the same. If you long to make an impact for Jesus in the twenty-first century, then this book is for you!'

Pastor Brian Houston, President, AOG Australia and Senior Pastor, Hillsong Church

SPECIAL THANKS

My very special thanks go to:

Davina, my fantastic wife and a true woman of God who lives Proverbs 31! This book is yet another result of your commitment to our call. None of the incredible things we've seen would have happened without you.

Deanna, a seventeen-year-old sweetheart who is already making God famous through her life, her music and her weekly radio programs.

Grant, a fourteen-year-old drummer who, when he's not drumming in church, loves to make TV, build websites and play Aussie rules football.

Jade, a twelve-year-old princess who loves to read her Bible, writes well and is the graphic artist of our family.

The committed team in our European office: Marcus Andersson, for your strong commitment to our mission; Marian King, for leaving a great country to help us in Europe; Tina and Rene Meyer, for all your creativity and devotion to our TV work; Dean Worth, for seeing the Internet as a mission field.

Those who made this text into a book: Hanne Andreasen for your invaluable work on typesetting and design; Jørgen Vium Olesen, Anthony Höglind, and all the team at Scandinavia Publishing, Denmark, for helping us to get this into print.

Our special co-workers and partners across Europe, especially: Jarle and Merete Tangstad and the team at Copenhagen Pentecostal Church, for your vision for culture; Ray Bevan, Stuart Bell, Karl-Axel Mentzoni, John Angelina, Scott Wilson, Gary Clarke, Andrew Owen and Gunnar Swahn, for standing behind us as you do (you are leaders who see the future before it happens).

All our great faith partners in Australia and beyond, particularly: Danny Guglielmucci, Gary Rucci, and the team at Southside Christian Centre, for your help in lifting Europe's spiritual profile in the land of my birth.

My family in Australia and my many wonderful friends around the world: you inspire me as you make God famous!

Mal Fletcher
July 2001

MAKING
GOD
FAMOUS

1

THE END

*It's December 31, 1999. We're on the cusp of a new
millennium. All over the world, people are going the
extra mile to celebrate this very special, once-in-a-
lifetime New Year's eve.*

*I'm tuned to CNN, watching the fireworks displays
from across the globe. I'm watching at home in Europe,
a long way from the land of my birth. All national
pride aside, I can't help thinking that the most
impressive display is the one lighting up the sky over
Sydney harbour.*

*The show costs three million dollars. The whole
thing goes on for an extravagant twenty-three minutes
- an amazing display of colour and sound. Finally,
when the last fireworks have exploded overhead and
the smoke is slowly starting to clear, there is just one
word showing in lights across the great length of the
Harbour Bridge. It's written in a beautiful calligraphic
style - the word 'Eternity'.*

In the middle of last century, a strange thing took
place each morning on the pavements and roads in and
around Sydney. People would be catching the train to
work, or walking to the office, when their eyes would be
arrested by a single word written in beautiful script on
the pavements underfoot. The word provoked questions
in their minds, questions about the meaning of life and
the destiny of the human soul. The word was loaded with
implications; the word was 'Eternity'.

For years, the identity of the writer was a mystery.
Nobody could catch him at it. Yet, as surely as the sun
rose the word would appear each day to make people
think and wonder.

For thirty-seven years, the word appeared across the city and suburbs - sometimes in the most unlikely places (even on the inside of a huge bell). It appeared over half a million times in all! Finally, the enigmatic scribbler was identified. Though he had always shunned publicity, he now told his story.

Years before, as a returned World War 1 soldier, he'd been an alcoholic. He'd grown up in poverty. His parents and siblings were all alcoholics and his sisters operated brothels. He had supported himself by stealing what he needed and visited prisons many times from the age of fifteen.

One day, he heard the message about Jesus - not religion, not church dogma, but Jesus. He committed his future to Christ.

Through God's power, he overcame his addiction to alcohol and was soon in regular employment. He asked God to help him point the way to Christ. He wanted to make people consider their status before God, to think about the kingdom of God.

After hearing a fiery Baptist preacher give a powerful sermon about heaven and hell, a strange idea came to him. He would take a piece of white chalk and write one word on the streets of his city, a word that would put life in perspective and point men and women to God. People rich and poor, small and great saw his handiwork, always rendered in chalk or crayon and always written at night so that he would not become a celebrity. He wanted to remain in the shadows to better point the way to his Lord.

He didn't hold a high position in society or in the church, yet his simple message provoked many thousands during his lifetime to think about their eternal souls. He would never have dreamed that years after his death, his little word would be reproduced in lights across the Sydney Harbour Bridge - and this time multiplied millions of TV viewers around the world would be made to ponder where they stood in the eyes of God.

What was this humble little man doing with his piece of chalk? *He was making God famous!*

More Famous Than God?

We're living in the age of webs you can surf on, sheep you can clone and chips you can't eat. Yet, if the Gallup polls are anything to go by, millions of people still believe in the existence of God. They want to believe that there might be someone up there who does hear us when we pray - and might be willing to help us.

After a century in which materialism and rationalism seemed to have put God to rest, many people in the western world today are not only open to the idea that there may be a God; they're positively curious about what he might be like.

In the closing days of the last century, one of television's most watched series was the ubiquitous *X-Files*. It suggested that there might be a truth that is 'out there' - beyond the reach of science and technology. A generation of young adults - members of the so-called 'Generation X' - were hooked by the series, because they liked the idea that we are not simply the sum total of our physical parts. Living in a post-modern age, they related to the notion that we are not machines living in a mechanistic universe, that there is more to life than meets the eye.

The producer of the series, Chris Carter, is reported to have said, 'I am a non-religious person looking for a religious experience.' All over the developed world, Carter is among friends.

At the same time, it must be said that the emerging generations know even less about the God of the Bible than did their parents (and *they* didn't know much).

In the late 90s, one of the Gallagher brothers from the British band *Oasis* was reported to have said that, as far as young people were concerned, his group had become more popular than God. Of course, he was echoing the words of John Lennon who happened to be one of his heroes. He might, however, also have been stating a fact.

If you ask most young adults in western countries, 'Whom do you think about the most - the heroes of the pop culture or the God of the Bible?' most will not answer, 'the God of the Bible'. Nightclubs attract more attention than churches and God just doesn't figure in everyday life or thinking all that much.

Whatever Happened To God?

For almost two thousand years, the history of Christianity's spread across the world was the story of European Christians. The only reason the world heard the message about Jesus was that European Christians prayed, planned, preached and often laid down their lives for their faith. Christian missionaries, explorers and ministers from Europe carried with them a redeeming message of love and hope that could be applied in every culture. It changed for the better the destiny of nations.

Meanwhile, back home, the civilising influence of Christian teaching was the major factor in the development of European societies. In fact, Christianity kept western civilisation alive during some of Europe's darkest days. Christian pioneers like Ireland's St. Patrick did more than build monasteries; they brought prosperity and peace to Europe. Because of their influence, warriors in the post Roman age exchanged their weapons for tools and trades. Even the savage barbarians were eventually converted, and Europe began to flourish.

Through the centuries that followed, Christianity enriched and elevated European life like nothing else. Look at the arts, for example. Master composers like Bach, Handel, Haydn, Mendelssohn and Dvorak and writers like Dante, Milton, Donne and Dostoyevsky all used their faith as the foundation for their work.

In the visual arts, painters like Da Vinci, Rembrandt, Rubens and Van Gogh often expressed Christian ideas, and there's no denying the influence of Christianity on Europe's finest architecture - the work of men like Michelangelo, Alberti and Brunelleschi, to name just a few.

Christian faith also lifted Europe's political and economic life. Christianity taught a respect for authority structures - even secular ones - and this gave stability to Western societies. When the Reformation came along, it brought with it a whole new work ethic: a respect for work as a gift from God. This was the fuel behind the industrial revolution and it created a political climate where free democracies could thrive.

European Christianity also led to the birth of modern scientific method. Christians taught that God is a rational person. If that is true, then it followed that his creation must be built on orderly principles, principles that can be uncovered and represented as scientific laws. Christianity also gave Europe its first schools and universities, and churches were always at the forefront of social welfare, launching the first feeding programs and international charities.

Question: Without Christianity, where would western civilisation be today? Answer: It probably wouldn't exist at all.

Yet many post-modern westerners see the church as an institution belonging to a distant time, something that's passed its 'use by' date. In Latin America right now, according to leading missiologists, 30,000 people become Christians every day. In China, the number is 20,000 and in Africa 15,000. Yet, in Europe, thousands of people every week leave the established church.

Whatever happened to God in the west?

'God Is Dead - And We Have Killed Him.'

The slide away from Christianity started in Europe a couple of centuries ago, during a period known as the Enlightenment. Just how enlightening it actually was, is a matter for debate. Around that time, many philosophers, scientists and artists began to promote a naturalistic world-view that left no room for God.

Charles Darwin gave us the idea that human beings are little more than monkeys who got lucky, gorillas who're having a 'good hair day'. Darwin's theories became popular with many people not because there was a mountain of evidence to support them - there's still *no* 'missing link' to show that one species can evolve from a different one - but because they seemed to offer a way of explaining human origins without God. Or, that's what people thought. In fact, even scientists today are asking the question, 'What happened *before* the Big Bang?'

This kind of godless naturalism became all the rage among European thinkers. In Germany, Frederick Nietzsche taught that 'God is dead and we have killed him.' He demanded that we reject Christian virtues like humility, kindness and charity, which he considered weak, and begin the process of creating a stronger human super-race - an idea the Nazi's later grabbed, with pleasure.

In France, Jean-Jacques Rousseau developed a philosophy where the state takes the place of God. The state, he said, is the true liberator of mankind, because it combines the basic goodness of many individual human wills into one great 'General Will'. Karl Marx also believed that the State should step in where God once reigned. There are no universal moral truths, he said, and the state must decide what is right and wrong. Religion and morality, he said, are simply systems used by one class of people to repress another.

Western society, and Europe in particular, has learned at great cost that the grandiose utopian ideas of people like Nietzsche, Rousseau and Marx just don't work. In fact, they've often led to absolute *disaster.* Around the world, tyrants of all shapes and sizes have used utopian concepts to defend oppression, murder and ethnic cleansing.

Looking at the mess springing up around them, Europe's philosophers eventually looking for a positive outlook for the future. That paved the way for twentieth century existentialism of writers like Jean-Paul Sartre. It says that life is meaningless and the best we can do is enjoy it and then embrace death. Just live for the moment and hope for the best. There's no purpose in our pain, and no hope of ultimate salvation. The past is irrelevant, and the future is uncertain, so we should just live for the moment. Don't think too much about the long-term or generational consequences of your actions, just wrap yourself in the experience of the now.

Meanwhile, science has tried to take the place of philosophy as the thing to give us hope. Yet today, technology is *raising* more questions than it's answering. As the Catholic writer and social commentator Jacques Ellul once said, 'We build faster and faster machines to take us nowhere.'

Why Be A Christian?

Ellul made another insightful statement. He said we live in a world where everything is means and there are no ends. Ours is world in which very few people stop to ask themselves where modern values and technology might be taking us. Hardly anybody, in the midst of the many changes we are making to our world, stops to ask the big question, 'Why?'

If you're a believer in Jesus, a true life-and-death, I'll-do-anything-you-want-of-me-Lord Christian, it's worth asking yourself that same question. Why *are* you a Christian? Is it because your grandmother had faith? Is it all the result of some genetic inclination toward religion? Or is it an environment thing: are you a Christian because your parents brought you - or dragged you - to church when you were a kid? Or perhaps it's just that you once fell in love with a Christian and have stayed ever since.

According to the Bible, the bottom line is this: you're a Christian because *God called you.* Jesus did to you what he did to his first followers - he said, 'Follow me!' It was the most fantastic invitation ever offered.

In one of my earlier books, *Get Real!,* I recalled my least favourite class in school: Physical Education, or 'PE' for short.[1] It wasn't that I hated sport, it was just that every week we had to endure a strange tribal ritual called 'Choosing Teams'.

No matter what team sport we were playing, the process always started the same way. Two of the biggest Arnold Stationwagon look-a-likes in the school would be appointed team captains. They would then get to choose from the rest of us mere mortals who would have the honour of joining their respective teams.

It always seemed to end the same way, too: my friends and I, proud members of the school chess team, were left languishing pitifully until last. On the outside we tried to appear nonchalant, but inside we were secretly screaming, 'Pick me! Pick me!' It wasn't fun. PE class only lasted for a couple of hours a week, yet to this day one of the most vivid memories from my school days is that feeling of not being chosen for the team.

When I later became a Christian and started to really investigate the Bible, I found to my great surprise that I had now been picked for the team of all teams! God himself had singled me out for special attention and recruited me for *his* cause.

What an invitation! It's one you and I share. But 'follow me' is also a command. My friend Winkie Pratney loves to point out that, 'The trouble with this Jesus is, he behaves like he's *God* or something!' Jesus calls you and me and expects us to promptly drop everything and follow. He doesn't play 'Who wants to be a millionaire?' or 'Let's make a deal'. He just gives this one quiet and confident command.

You see, the initiative in your becoming a Christian was God's, not yours. *He* started the process - for a reason. So, why *did* God call you to be a Christian? What is the 'end' of your Christian faith? What is the reason for your being a Christian, and what is the goal?

According to the Bible, the major reason God calls a people to himself is to *make a great name for himself.* It's a theme repeated many times throughout the Bible. In the Old Testament for example, the people of Israel were constantly reminded that God had set them apart from other nations and had given them a special calling, because he wanted to exalt his name through them, to show all the earth what he is like.

Israel's greatest Old Testament king, David, recognised this. He prayed:

> 'And who is like your people Israel - the one nation on earth whose God went out to redeem a people for himself, and to make a name for yourself, and to perform great and awesome wonders by driving out nations from before your people, whom you redeemed from Egypt?' (1 Chronicles 17:21)

One of Israel's most distinguished prophets saw it too:

> '[God] sent his glorious arm of power to be at Moses' right hand, [he] divided the waters before [Israel] to gain for himself everlasting renown.' (Isaiah 63:12)

This same idea is given many times in the Old Testament: God wants to be a 'household name', he wants to gain for himself a special renown.[2]

In the New Testament, we find a similar theme. The Lord's Prayer, for example, begins with a call for God's name to be 'hallowed', a word that means to set something above the commonplace, to make it special.[3] The apostle Paul tells us that, in eternity, we will be God's personal trophies, showing all that his grace has done.[4]

We're told it's the number one reason we pray, and the major purpose for evangelism.[5] We share the gospel and disciple others not primarily to see them saved - that's the *fruit* of evangelism. The *motive* for evangelism is that we want to honour God's name!

God wants to become a household name or, in modern terms, *God wants to be famous!*

What On Earth Is God Up To?

I visit around twenty countries every year, some of them more than once, on at least four continents. There's one piece of news I can give you that you won't catch on CNN. God *is* making himself famous around the globe today.

Down through the years, Palermo, Sicily is a part of Italy that's been known for just one thing: Al Pacino movies. It's the world headquarters for Mafia Inc., the home of the Godfathers. It hasn't been a real hotbed of godliness!

Around ten years ago, God spoke to a friend of mine and told him to start a church in this seemingly God-forsaken place. Lirio Porrello is a medical doctor - not necessarily the first choice for a church planter, you may think. In simple obedience, and without much experience of church leadership, Lirio started his church.

Today in Palermo, there is a church of over three thousand people. It's a church where sick bodies are healed, where oppressing demons are cast out of people's lives and where the Word of God is preached without fear or compromise. Some of the members of the church are ex-Mafia people. Some of the younger leaders were once skinhead neo-Nazis who spray-painted Jewish graves just for fun. Today, these men and women have been radically transformed by the love of Christ and they're leading other young people to faith. This church is having an influence in a spiritually dry area. What's it called when churches start reforming cities? It's called *making God famous!*

The Rhema church, in Johannesburg, South Africa, is made up of twenty thousand people. It was started by a former champion body-builder, Ray McCauley, when the old apartheid regime was at its strongest. A few years ago, I was asked to be one of the speakers at an international conference run by this great church. People came from all over the nation and far beyond.

The event kicked off with a rather unusual meeting. The music was in full swing when Nelson Mandela, then the president of the nation, made his way into a packed auditorium. Surrounded by thousands of people, among them a large contingent of security and media personnel, the president danced with the children. Then, he was introduced as the speaker for the session.

President Mandela, a world icon, a symbol of the power of right to overthrow wrong, shared from a pulpit for almost half an hour. He talked about how this church, and the Christian faith, had helped him overcome bitterness in the wake of his long imprisonment. What's it called when a church influences presidents? It's called *making God famous*!

Not too long ago, Michael Jackson conducted a world tour. In almost every city he visited, he filled football stadiums with his fans. There was one notable exception: the city of Seoul, South Korea. Michael couldn't fill the stadium, but a few weeks after he left, the same venue was booked for a totally different purpose.

Dr. David Yonghi Cho hired the stadium - and filled it - for a *prayer meeting*! No, not a conference, a concert or a festival, but a prayer meeting. What's it called when Christians pack football stadiums that rock 'gods' can't fill? It's called *making God famous*!

It's not just the big churches who are making God a name, either. I have a friend in Sweden who leads a church of two hundred people - in a town of just two thousand! Fifty of the two hundred members of Joshua Christian Centre are employed full-time in various community projects run by the church. The church owns, among other things, a brand new home for the aged, apartment buildings and a school, as well as the worship centre itself.

Not long ago, a stranger was trying to find his way around town. A little lost, he pulled his car to the side of the road and asked a passer-by: 'Can you tell me where to find Joshua Christian Centre?' The local, not a churchgoer himself, replied, 'Look around you - they're everywhere!'

What's it called when a small church represents ten percent of the city's population, and owns much of its property? It's called *making God famous*!

Today, God is raising up churches and evangelistic and missions organisations that have just one objective in mind: to make his name great. He is pouring out his Spirit on generations of Christian people from every tribe, language and nation; bringing together a people who care only about one thing. They will live and die to *make God famous.*

God Wants To Be Famous ... So What?

Why does God want his name to be known? If I told you I want to be famous, you might say, 'This guy has a serious ego problem,' or, 'This guy is insecure'. And you might well be right. So, is God feeling insecure ('Quick Gabriel, get some posters out - people have forgotten I exist')? Does God have an ego problem?

No, God wants to be famous not for his sake but for *mine.* You see, if we lose respect for God's name, or his nature and character, there are three things that will follow.

1. We forget what God is like.

According to the Bible, unless we know what God is like we cannot hope to exercise faith in him, to reach out to him and connect with him. The writer of the book of Hebrews says this:

'And without faith it is impossible to please God, because anyone who comes to him must believe that he exists and that he rewards those who earnestly seek him.'
(Hebrews 11:6)

Whoever comes to God for anything must first believe that God exists. But what kind of God, (after all, there are so many variations on the theme)? Answer: God as he is described in the Bible.

The core of the whole Bible is that the God who is *transcendent* - way beyond our ability to comprehend - wants to be *immanent*, he wants to reveal himself to us in ways we can understand. Unless he takes that initiative we would have no hope of ever having any relationship with him.

So, how does God reveal himself to us? Partly through the names he has given himself, names that tell us something of his nature and character. More on that in a moment...

2. We build idols to take God's place.

Whether we like it or not, we human beings were wired to look for a God. As one writer said, 'There's a God-shaped hole in every human heart.' At some time in our lives, every one of us will try to fit something or some-one into that space. Something or someone will become the object of our greatest affection and devotion.

It may be an idea. It might be another person - a marriage partner or a friend. Or, perhaps a dream or a goal - that career promotion, for example, or a bigger bank balance. It may even be a physical object - a piece of property, a car or a boat.

Whatever I make my 'god' will significantly shape my destiny, becoming a focus for my sense of meaning. That person, goal or thing will affect my future more than anything else will, because I will make decisions with him, her, or it, uppermost in my mind.

Again, that's a reflection of the way we were made. We were made to live 'in the image' of our God.[6] If the true God is not god of our lives, then we will inevitably find ourselves being shaped by those things or people that *are* most important to us.

3. We miss our destiny.

Whether our idols are made of wood and stone, or plastic and steel; whether they are the dreams of scientists or the ideals of utopian philosophers, they will dethrone God in our hearts. They will make him less than he should be in our lives and, in the process, they will reduce *us*.

What is the end result of placing anything above God? The apostle Paul again:

> *'For although they knew God, they neither glorified him as God nor gave thanks to him, but their thinking became futile and their foolish hearts were darkened. Although they claimed to be wise, they became fools and exchanged the glory of the immortal God for images made to look like mortal man and birds and animals and reptiles.' (Romans 1:21-23)*

The end result of placing anything above God is that our thinking becomes 'futile' - empty, meaningless and vain. Simply put, we become useless when compared to what God had originally planned for our lives. We can no longer live up to the wonderful purpose for which we were first created, because that purpose was based on our being in relationship with the Creator.

In a sense, that's what hell is, a place for people whose lives have been wasted as far as God's plans were concerned. That's why when Jesus spoke of hell - and for him it was a very real place - he often used the picture of 'Gehenna', a valley outside Jerusalem where people used to dump and burn their waste.[7]

Many people living in Europe around the time of the Enlightenment must have thought that by turning their backs on Christianity, they'd be free to do as they please. In fact, they simply replaced the God of their fathers with other gods that aren't real. In Paul's words, they simply 'exchanged the truth of God for a lie, and worshiped and served created things rather than the Creator.'[8]

According to the Bible, a human life begins to unravel when we forget what our Creator is like. Nietzsche ended his days in an insane asylum, dying with syphilis. He not only preached that God is dead; he set out to live as if it were true, spending much of his time partying with prostitutes. When you give up on God, and set out to live as if he does not exist, you become a candidate for despair.

Rousseau's godless philosophy taught that, among other things, the responsibility for the raising of children should be taken from parents and handed to the state. His philosophy was, in fact, a rationalisation for the careless and godless way in which he lived. A committed Bohemian, he went from job to job and mistress to mistress, until he finally settled with a young servant girl, called Terese. She bore him five children, all of whom he abandoned on the steps of orphan houses. For those children, in those times, this meant a life of trying to find food on the streets. Rousseau knew full well that this was basically a death sentence.

If we live as if there is no God, we don't elevate human nature; we plumb its darkest depths.

What is true for an individual is also, ultimately, true for a society. When a nation tries to replace faith in God with faith in human leaders, or human systems, it unleashes the very *worst* in human nature. Western civilisation's modern history bears this out.

What happened in Germany and Italy in the days preceding World War 2, for example, was not just the result of certain political or military phenomena. It was a direct result of once great bastions of Christianity turning their backs on God. There is a clear philosophical lineage linking, for example, Nietzsche's 'super race' and Hitler. Nietzsche might have been horrified to see what Hitler did with his ideas, but the fact remains that they *could* easily be used to justify ethnic cleansing.

Our sin, our fallenness from God's original plan, has made a separation between us and our God.[9] It has often blurred our view of God - smeared the windscreen of our minds, and made us lose sight of the right road ahead.

What's In A Name?

To teach us what he is like, the God of the Bible has constantly and progressively uncovered to us aspects of his nature and character. From earliest Bible times, God was revealing himself through the names he gave for himself. By teaching people to call him by those names, he developed and reinforced their understanding of his nature and character.

Very early in the human story, men like Abraham were calling God by the name *Adonay* or *Adonai*, which is usually translated *Lord* and means ruler or sovereign.[10] Then, God invited them to call him *El Shaddai*. Though it is often translated *God Almighty*, it actually means the all-sufficient God, the one who has everything we need and more.[11]

Later, Israel knew God by names like *Jehovah Jireh* (the God who will provide),[12] and *Jehovah Shalom* (the God who sends peace).[13]

There were many other names too, each one reflecting a particular truth about his character.[14] It's not that each new name superseded the last, it's just that each one added something which gave people a fuller understanding of who God is. In fact, the very word *God* as it is used in the Bible is a special one. It literally means the 'Supreme God', the one and only God who is God by nature. In other words, he is God whether we choose to acknowledge it or not.

Now, it's not the names that are powerful, it's the Person to whom they point us. God's favourite means of communication is incarnation. He loves to express himself first with pictures, with demonstrations of what he is like.

The names God gave himself were in fact his first incarnations. They are phrases God chose to incarnate his nature, to describe his character in terms we can understand. Before we had the Bible, we had God's names to show us who he is. Before we had the person of Jesus - the ultimate incarnation of God - we had those names to remind us what he's like.

Whenever God introduced himself by a new name, it was for a purpose: there was always a 'pay off' in the lives of the people to whom he gave the name. When God introduced himself to Abraham as *El Shaddai*, it was to give Abraham the faith to believe the awesome promise God was making him.[15]

To Moses, God introduced himself as the *I AM*.[16] For anyone else, *I AM* would be an unfinished sentence, a preposition lacking a noun or an adjective. For God, however, it *is* the sentence. It's a complete description of who God is, it is a name for God. Why did Moses need this name? Because he needed enormous courage to face the wrath of Pharaoh.

God was saying this to Pharaoh: 'You may say, "I am a great king", but if it weren't for who I AM, there would be no kings. I AM the "king of kings".'

'You may say, "I represent a great nation", but if it wasn't for who I AM, there would be no nations. I draw up the boundaries and set the times and seasons for nations.'

'You may call yourself all kinds of things, but they will all ultimately spring out of who I AM. You may have a name, but I am the preposition that proceeds all names: you cannot be what you are unless I am what I AM!'

God was reminding Pharaoh - and Moses - just who was boss! God's names can still teach us a great deal about him and, in the process, give us courage to face our own Pharaohs.

More Famous Than John Lennon...

In the New Testament, we have the greatest of all names for God; the one we're told will ultimately be *the* most famous, throughout eternity. It's the name of Jesus.

To Peter, God revealed himself as, 'the Christ, the Son of the living God.'[17] Jesus, God in the flesh, was the ultimate revelation of God to humankind. The name of Jesus is the greatest of all the names we have for God.

That's why Jesus said Peter's confession was the rock on which he would build his church.[18] The Christian church, which has withstood so many fierce attacks and persecutions through the centuries, is still standing strong and continues to grow throughout the world - especially the developing world - today. Why? Because the church is not built on the quality of its worship, the power of its preaching or the relevance of its social programs. The church is built on the authority of Jesus' name, the authority of who he is.

Paul told us that God has made Jesus' name more powerful than any other name. Paul wrote these immortal words, which some authorities believe belong to an early Christian hymn:

> 'God exalted [Jesus] to the highest place and gave him the name that is above every name, that at the name of Jesus every knee should bow, in heaven and on earth and under the earth, and every tongue confess that Jesus Christ is Lord, to the glory of God the Father.' (Philippians 2:9-11)

Whenever something great happens in the name of Jesus, God is glorified, honoured or 'made famous'. In every culture, among every race and ethnic group, the name of Jesus has a special power. Prayer in his name often results in the healing of sick bodies. It brings rest to troubled minds. It heals damaged relationships.

When we pray in the authority of Jesus' name, we can reap the same results today as he did two thousand years ago. All over the world, every day, there are millions of miracles, large and small, that attest to the power of this name.

Every time any one of us receives an answered prayer in Jesus' name, we are revealing something about God and making him known to a generation who thinks he's forgotten them - because they've often forgotten him.

When we pray for healing in Jesus' name and a person is healed, we're showing that our God is a healer. When we pray about a financial situation in Jesus' name and we receive the money we need, we're demonstrating that our God is a provider. Whenever Christians gather to worship in the name of Jesus, they bring the special presence of God's Holy Spirit - an atmosphere of God's beauty and power.

More Than A Name!

I was in Canada speaking at a conference. It was set in a hotel overlooking the incredible Niagara Falls and Gen-X adults had gathered from right across the Toronto region for what turned out to be a powerful series of meetings.

The guy leading the conference, Dave, was a friend of mine. All weekend he and his team had experienced strong opposition from the manager of the hotel. It seemed she couldn't open her mouth to him without complaining about something - usually something insignificant. Dave couldn't understand why she was so 'aggro' in her attitude. It didn't matter what he was doing, she managed to find fault with it, right down to the smallest details. In the end, he could only explain her attitude as a spiritual thing - she just had a problem with Christians, period.

On the main night of the event, he stood at the back of the auditorium watching as the Holy Spirit began to move among the people. God was doing some great things in people's lives, following the preaching of his word. Out of the corner of his eye, Dave saw the manager approaching him. He thought, 'Here we go again. I don't need this right now.' He tried to avoid her eye, but she came up and positioned herself right in front on him.

He waited for the hammer to drop, but she just stood there for a moment while tears welled up in her eyes. Then she said, very quietly and with feeling: 'There's some very positive energy in this room, isn't there?'

That young hotel manager didn't know what to call it; she wasn't familiar with the terms like 'the presence of God', or 'the anointing of the Holy Spirit'. But she knew she was experiencing something - or someone - special in that room. She was in the presence of a King! She could sense a change in the spiritual atmosphere, because Christians were gathered in Jesus' name, worshipping him and lifting up his name.

So, the name of Jesus is a special name. But it's not the word 'Jesus' itself that is especially powerful. Even today, in many parts of the world, you'll come across thousands of baby boys who are given that name. If you pray using the name of any of these children, absolutely nothing will happen, even if they're great kids!

It's not the *word* 'Jesus' that has power; it's the moral and spiritual excellence, and the position of the person behind the name! It's the nature of Christ and his authority as God's risen Son that makes prayer, faith and action in his name such an awesome thing.

God wants his *name* to be known, to be great, because he wants to demonstrate to people everywhere what he is like. Only then will they know how to respond to him, how to enjoy his friendship, how to connect with him and how to please him.

The question for this book is this: how do we make God's name great again in *our* age, in this post-modern western world which has been so affected by humanism, rationalism and live-today-die-tomorrow existentialism. How do we make God famous in *our* time, where *we* live?

1. *Get Real!* is now available as an e-book at www.nextwaveinternational.com
2. See, for example, 1 Kings 8:41-43 and 2 Chronicles 7:14
3. Matthew 6:9
4. Ephesians 2:6-7
5. Matthew 6:9 and John 15:8
6. Genesis 1:26-27
7. Mark 9:47
8. Romans 1:25
9. Isaiah 59:2
10. Genesis 18:27
11. Genesis 17:1
12. Genesis 22:14
13. Judges 6:24
14. For example, *Jehovah Nissi* (the Lord my banner - Exodus 17:15) and *Jehovah Tsidkenu* (the Lord who is our righteousness - Jeremiah 23:6)
15. Genesis 17:1-8
16. Exodus 3:14
17. Matthew 16:18
18. Ibid.

2

Bigger Than Babylon

You're fit, well educated and your mind is filled with great dreams for the future.

One day, as you sit in a university lecture or business seminar, the doors of the room are kicked in by a group of gun-toting warriors dressed in battle fatigues. You and your colleagues are pushed at gunpoint into a large unmarked truck that's been driven straight through the front wall of the building. From there, you're driven to a local airport where, with guns still pointed in your direction, you are rushed onto a waiting plane. While you're still trying to gather your thoughts and come to grips with what is happening, the plane takes off. Many hours later, you and your friends find yourselves sitting in a dungeon somewhere under Tianneman Square.

Nearly twenty-four hours after your abduction, you discover that you are now an official houseguest of the Chinese red army - and that they don't plan on sending you back. They intend to indoctrinate you with Communist Party dogma. They're going to change your diet, your clothing, even your name, in an effort to integrate you into Chinese life and customs.

How do you feel right now? Are you afraid, frustrated, or angry? You probably feel much the same as a prince called Daniel did in ancient times.

Even as a young man, Nebuchadnezzar, king of Babylon, was a skilled and shrewd conqueror. He had learned from history that to crush nationalistic spirit in the people you conquer only leads to rebellion and revolution somewhere down the track.

Rather than kill the national pride of his captives, he tried to totally integrate them, over time, into

Babylonian life - to make them see themselves as Babylonian. To do this, he would always start with young adults, people who were still open to new experiences and impressions yet educated enough to understand the subtleties of Babylonian literature and science. The process of integration began with the removal of certain things.

Once Babylon had people in its sights, it would strip them of their homes, language, literature, food and names.[1] Every one of these things represented an important aspect of their sense of identity.

Nebuchadnezzar's strategy was to totally alienate people from their roots, from all association with their previous identities, and integrate them into an alien system. He sought to build into them a new identity of his own making.

In Daniel's case, he and his friends were well aware that their nation had been promised a special place as God's set-apart people. God had promised Israel a unique identity among the nations.[2] All the other promises God made to this people flowed out of this one. If Israel's role among the nations could be compromised, the world would lose its major opportunity up to that point to see what God is like, and to reach out to him. [3]

Babylon Revisited

Babylon is alive and well today. Not the physical city - that's a wasteland as the Bible predicted it would be:

> '"Before your eyes I will repay Babylon and all who live in Babylonia for all the wrong they have done in Zion," declares the LORD. "I am against you, O destroying mountain, you who destroy the whole earth," declares the LORD. "I will stretch out my hand against you, roll you off the cliffs, and make you a burned-out mountain. No rock will be taken from you for a cornerstone, nor any stone for a foundation, for you will be desolate forever," declares the LORD.'
> (Jeremiah 51:24-26)

On several occasions, Saddam Hussein has tried to rebuild the ancient city, the site of which now lies in Iraq. He has always met with failure, because God has declared it will be desolate, or totally empty, forever.

It's the *spirit* of the Babylon that is still around today. In the Bible, Babylon is not simply a physical entity; its name is used metaphorically as well. In the New Testament, the word 'Babylon' refers to any world system of government or thinking which seeks to usurp the place of Christ as King of Kings.[4] It refuses to accept God's moral law and tries to make something or someone else lord of the earth. Because it tries to take the place of Jesus, building a world kingdom without its rightful king, it is called is an 'anti-Christ' system. One day it will be overseen by a powerful human leader whom the Bible calls *the* Antichrist because he will embody in one person everything for which this Babylon stands.[5]

The original version of the name Babylon is linked with the biblical Tower of Babel, a multi-storeyed tower that was intended to be a contact point between men and pagan gods. Men wanted to make a name for themselves rather than God and their tower attracted the judgement of God and was destroyed.[6] 'Babel' literally means 'confusion' and, as with the ancient tower, Babylon typifies the confusion that results when human beings try to build God's good kingdom without God.

The Living Computer Virus

A computer virus creates nothing new. It simply corrupts what someone else has created. Once a virus gets into your computer, it prevents you from receiving any of the benefits you should get from using programs. Satan is like a computer virus. Only God can create anything *ex nihilo* - from nothing. The devil simply tries to corrupt what God is doing. He tries to stop you enjoying any of the good things you can receive from God's promises.

Satan's strategy for the generations of our time is the same as the one he used in Daniel's day. He tries to alienate people from their sense of being set apart by God. He works to integrate them into a way of life that allows no room for God or his plans and so brings people out of any covenant relationship with their Creator. When that happens they can enjoy none of the promises God has made them in the Scriptures.

Daniel 1:1 says that Babylon's forces 'besieged' the city of Jerusalem. We, too, are living in an age where people feel besieged. Many people, of all ages, feel increasingly confused by the rapid changes taking place around them. We are bombarded with so many new choices and options that we're often left wondering where we really fit in. As one Gen-Xer put it, 'We're not out to destroy the system. We just can't find our place in it!'

In our times, we've seen the emergence of the 'whatever' generations. That word has become a catch-cry for Generation X and Generation Next. What message does it convey? It says, 'Don't tell me what you want to do, or what you want me to do. I'm overloaded with choices here. I don't have the energy to get involved.'

The Babylon in which we live tries to undermine our sense of being chosen by God for a unique purpose. It does so by attacking the same five things that attracted Nebuchadnezzar's attention.

Home

Today, the very definition of 'family' is under fire. Talk of so-called 'gay' couples adopting children is no longer shocking news. Not all homosexuals are gay - the word means happy, light-hearted and carefree. Many despise a lifestyle that they intuitively feel is unnatural, but which seems to have them trapped.

The thing people forget about human sin - abandoning God's ways for our own moral constructs - is that it always takes you further than you wanted to go. What is considered firm and unquestionable in this generation will, if we keep rejecting God's will, become totally negotiable in the next. What we consider over-the-top today may very well become acceptable, even desirable, tomorrow.

Some people in the 60s - and it certainly *wasn't* everybody - believed the world needed a 'sexual revolution'. They advocated a lifestyle where commitment in a sexual relationship was just an optional extra. The buzzwords were 'free love'. Yet, many of those very same people today are dismayed or unsettled by the idea that homosexual couples are allowed to adopt children. They know that this is a threat to the very foundations on which society is built.

It may not be pleasant to think about, but who's to say that a future generation - and one not too far away - won't wonder why we all have such a 'hang up' about incest? If we've already accepted that consenting adults should have the right to do pretty much what they want with each other sexually, why rule out consenting sex between adult brothers and sisters? As I write this, news reports are emerging about the first ever case of artificial insemination involving a brother and sister. Once you abandon the idea that there is an absolute right and wrong, you leave yourself open to abuses like this.

When a generation loses its sense of family, it loses one of the most important building blocks for human identity. It is from the balance of the family unit that we first begin to understand our place in the world: sexually, emotionally and socially. In the family, we first experience the all-important elements of a healthy self-esteem: the sense that we are worthy of love, the sense that we belong, and the sense that we can contribute something worthwhile to people around us.

A society that loses its sense of family also gives up an important part of its knowledge of God. One of the most powerful things we can know about God is that he is, by nature, a Father - a Father who loved us so much that he sent us his only Son. Family expresses what God is like.

The human family is not a human construct - it is a divine gift. Family was God's idea. It was he who decided what the correct definition and structure of a family would be. It's something he revealed at the very beginning of our history.

A man would leave his own father and mother, God said, and 'be united with' - literally, inseparably 'glued' - to his wife.[7] They would leave behind their own families to form a new one. Their joining together would become something so intimate, so close, that to try to pull them apart would be like trying to separate two objects that had been super-glued together. Hence, the profound pain people experience during a divorce.

Strip away the family - as *God* defines it - and you mess with the minds and hearts of generations to come. We can make God famous by building great families.

Talk To Me...

When Babylon insisted Daniel must learn a new language, it was not simply giving him a free night school course in cross-cultural communication. It was changing the whole way Daniel and his friends related to other people.

What is language, is it just words and sentences? Is it just about building conversations? No, language is central to the way we build *relationships*. Babylon was attacking Daniel's means of forming friendships.

The Babylon of our time is putting enormous pressure on friendships and relationships. It's ironic that in the so-called 'age of communication' we have so many people feeling lonely and alienated from their fellow human beings. Partly, this has to do with the fracturing of the family which is where, ideally, we should first experience 'inherent-value love' - that is, love based not on what we can do, but on who we are.

Too much emphasis on individualism has also put a strain on our relationships. Dr. Carl Meninger said that sin is sacrificing the welfare of others for the satisfaction of the self. Today, that kind of attitude has been made into something of a virtue. We flaunt a 'Just-Do-It' mentality without thinking that our actions have consequences for others. We're proud to call ours a consumer society, ignoring the social problems that follow in the wake of this.

Jesus is the greatest example of a *non*-consumer in all of human history. He summed up his mission on earth with these words:

> 'For even the Son of Man did not come to be served, but to serve, and to give his life as a ransom for many.' (Mark 10:45)

Real love is not overly concerned with self because it's too busy looking out for the welfare of others. It gets more joy from giving than receiving. We're all self-interested, but there's a great difference between that and preoccupation with self. Somebody once said that it's hard to imagine Mother Teresa needing therapy; she was too busy searching out the needs of others to be preoccupied with her own insecurities.

Say the word 'love' and most people think of romance, of chemistry. Real love, however, is much more than an emotion. It's a powerful law or governing force that underlies the whole of God's universe. Jesus summed this up when he taught that the two greatest commandments are that you love God with all your heart, soul and mind, and that you love your neighbour as yourself.[8]

Notice which one he put first. Love for God is a moral imperative - that is, it's a fundamental principle on which the universe works. If we love God, we will live by his values and obey his instructions. As a result, we will live in harmony with other people and with the moral universe in which we live. What's more, loving God first in our lives will ennoble our goals and dreams, giving us the motivation and the courage to improve the lives of others.

Two very good friends of mine are well known in the fast growing field of Christian worship music. Darlene Zschech is the voice that drives the incredible Hillsong Music albums. Her song-writing and vocal skills are topped only by her love for worshipping God. Her husband Mark is a gifted entrepreneur, the business mind behind the Hillsong tours, and a man with a strong commitment to communicating Christ through the media.

A little while ago, they launched a new ministry, one that offers care and professional help to young women in crisis. They purchased a large house and transformed it from an empty building into a real home for women suffering all kinds of emotional disorders. To do this, they had to fight local council opposition to their dream. They had to raise sponsorship from business people and generous individuals. They had to invest their own money, time and energies, on top of all their other responsibilities in their church and ministry.

It would have been easy for Mark and Darlene to sit back and enjoy the fruits of their musical success. Instead, their love for God led them to take risks to rescue hurting people. [9]

That's what happens when you put love for God at the top of your priority list - you find that you are truly free to love others in a meaningful, practical way. We can make God famous by taking those kinds of risks born out of our love for God.

It's a Three-Way Street!

You don't need a master's degree in statistical analysis to recognise that many people in our western culture today are having trouble keeping marriages together. This is having a profound impact on the mental and physical well being of men, woman and children.

In the U.K., for example, the number of sole-parent families has increased dramatically in the past thirty years or so. Only eight percent of families had single parents in 1971, but by 1995 that number had climbed to twenty-one percent.[10] In that country, divorce is a major contributor to health problems among adults, and divorced men aged twenty-five to fifty are twice as likely as married men to die prematurely.[11] Admission rates to mental hospitals are four to six times greater among divorced people than married people, and divorced people smoke more, drink more, and have higher rates of unsafe sex than married people. They're also four times more likely to commit suicide.[12]

What about the children? Studies show that children from divorced families are more likely to have a higher incidence of a range of social, economic, psychological and physical health problems compared with children from intact families. They are also likely to struggle with key life changes and to have a greater chance of their own marriage ending in divorce.[13]

Now, it's worth remembering that God's power can change any situation for the better. You can be a single parent and raise healthy, well adjusted children. You can grow up in a single parent family and thrive in life. However, divorce seriously cuts down the odds in favour of a happy home and a healthy life.

The fact is, there wasn't a single ancient culture that did not know, appreciate and honour marriage - *and* protect it by law. This might suggest that the marriage bond between a man and a woman is more than just 'a cultural thing'. Perhaps it was more than just a human invention.

In the western world, our models for marriage and family have traditionally been based upon the teaching of the Judeo-Christian religious heritage and, more specifically, on the Bible. According to the Bible, marriage is a model handed down to us from the hand of God himself.[14] Marriage was God's idea, and it reflects something of his nature.

The word 'covenant' is one that has, sadly, been almost lost to everyday life, except perhaps as a piece of legal jargon. Yet, it was a word that meant a great deal to ancient cultures. It spoke of two friends, or even people groups, whose relationship had grown beyond the level of a normal friendship. They had come to the point where a special commitment was made - usually in very public ways. Covenant-makers would make a binding promise to stand up for each other, even if it cost them everything to do so. Covenant was always about putting the interests of the other party above one's own. By entering into a covenant, people were saying:

'When you are poor, I will provide for you. When you are weak, I will make you strong. If you are under attack, I will stand and fight for you, even if it costs me my life. And, if people give you up, if they discard you because you have made a mistake, I will lift you up again.'

Covenant has always been a powerful thing, a concept that has enriched societies and individual lives. The God of the Bible is a covenant-maker. He makes binding commitments in *our* best interests.

According to the Bible, marriage is a covenant. It is more than a social contract like buying a piece of land or getting a job.[15] People have often spoken of marriage as two people 'tying the knot'. In one way, though it's old fashioned to say it, that's not such a bad description. In Christian terms, marriage is about two people who become bound together in all sorts of interesting and personally fulfilling ways. When two people are married, they see a widening of their earning potential, their circle of friends, their recreational interests and much more.

Some people see the massive increase in marriage breakdown today, and they point an accusing finger at the church. 'See,' they say, 'The Christian view of marriage just doesn't work.' If you ask them, though, what they think *is* the Christian view of marriage, they'll say something like this: 'The Christian picture of marriage is two people living together for the rest of their lives.'

Actually, that has *never* been the complete Christian view of marriage. All human relationships were made to mirror the image of God himself. Our relationships were designed to honour God, by revealing what he is like.

It's a difficult concept for us to get our heads around, but the God of the Bible is a triune Being: Father, Son and Holy Spirit.[16] These three Persons of the eternal Godhead live in a perfect relationship of harmony, selflessness and love. Because we were created in God's image, even our relationships are meant to mirror God's nature and character. Our relationships are meant to be like his - three-way in nature. A friendship should be about two people *and God.* A business partnership should be about two people *and God.* Similarly, a marriage was never intended to just be about a man and wife. It was meant to be man, wife *and God.* Marriage is a binding promise of love, made between a man and a woman *and* between them and God (cf. Proverbs 2:17).

In all this, the Bible never asks us to build a marriage on duty alone. Covenants as important as marriage are held together not by law but by love. In fact, that's why marriage is so sacred, because it reflects something very important about the nature of God. In the words of the apostle John:

'God is love.' (1 John 4:8)

God does not just *feel* love, or *experience* it. He is the very *essence* of what we call love. Without him, there would be no love in the universe, because all love flows out of his nature. When we build relationships that work, we're showing everyone around us something of God's own nature - we're making him famous. The love commitment of marriage is a kind of revelation of the wonder of God's own nature.

That's why, the Bible says, God hates divorce.[17] In certain circumstances, God will, in his compassion and mercy, permit divorce when all else has failed. Yet, he is nowhere near as open to it as are our modern law books. Divorce hurts him and runs counter to everything he has built into his creation. As a result, it cannot help but hurt us too.

The love which holds a marriage together, the love of God, has nothing to do with the fickle love of the rock songs. That's something you 'fall in', and can 'fall out of' just as easily. Love is not an accident - it is a strong, enduring thing based on decision and commitment. Yes, of course there's chemistry in a successful marriage. What man or woman wants to spend the rest of his or her life with someone who's never 'flicked their switches'? But chemistry without commitment brings *crisis*. It may get you to the altar, but it won't carry you much further. On its own, romance can never bring the kind of fulfilment you experience when your relationship is built around honouring God. Sex is at its best when it is serving, not dominating, the friendship.

Babylon has robbed many people today of the ability to discover God's presence in their relationships. Their relationships suffer because God is not honoured in them.

You Are What You Eat

Daniel and his friends not only lost their homes and their language; they lost their normal diet as well. All over the world, even today, people love to define who they are by what they eat. Italians love their pasta and the English cherish their fish and chips. Texans brag (rightly) about their steaks and if you're an Aussie, like me, there are days when you hang out for a good meat pie!

In Daniel's case, of course, food was not just a cultural thing; it said something about the faith of his people. Moses' law had laid out some clear ideas on what was and what was not good to eat. These instructions on food weren't given just to protect the health of the people, but to set them apart from other nations as the special people of God. Their food was bound up with their cultural and spiritual identity.

Babylon removed this important expression of culture and faith; it tried to completely alter the way Daniel's generation related to their bodies. These days,

Babylon tries to squeeze us into one of two extremes. Either we worship the body, spending every spare minute in a gym trying to build up the perfect torso, or we totally ignore it, never bothering to look at what we're doing to it or what we're feeding into it.

If we fall into the first trap, we are forever placing the temporal over the eternal. Paul says this:

'For physical training is of some value, but godliness has value for all things, holding promise for both the present life and the life to come.' (1 Timothy 4:8)

He doesn't say that physical exercise is worthless. It's just that people are making a huge mistake when they are more concerned with their bodies - which, after all, are temporary - than with the state of their souls - which are eternal. If many of us invested as much time in exercising the soul and spirit - through prayer and worship, for example - as we do on building the body, our lives would truly make God famous.

People who fall into the second trap, ignoring the welfare of their bodies, are dishonouring the God who gave them this precious gift. They're also showing that an ungodly, destructive attitude has already taken root in their hearts. They're basically saying, 'What's the use of looking after me? I'm not worth anything.' That kind of attitude will always stop them reaching out for God's best in their lives.

One of the ways in which Babylon attacks our bodies is through the reliance it brings on drugs. In fact, we were warned about this in the Bible - long before we ever knew we *had* a drug problem!

The book of Revelation foresees the downfall of the new Babylon we see around us today. Speaking to Babylon, it says this:

'For your merchants were the great men of the earth, for by your sorcery all the nations were deceived.' (Rev. 18: 21-23)

That word 'sorcery' is actually a Greek word from which we get our words 'pharmacy' and 'pharmaceutical'. Winkie Pratney writes that, 'According to Scripture, the power of Babylon is *pharmakia*, the word translated "sorceries" or "witchcraft" - the thing that gives this principality its world power.'[18] Drugs are one of the major commercial powers behind Babylon.

In so many ways, ours *is* a drugged generation. It's not only illicit drugs that are a problem; it's those little everyday panacea we use to help us cope with life. Big drug companies show massive returns for their investors by inventing new drugs and then, through the power of advertising, encouraging us to make them a normal part of our lives. One consequence of our increased reliance on chemicals is that diseases we thought we had wiped out are now resurfacing. The bugs that cause them are developing immunities to our drugs.

For example, in 1989 it was impossible to find one case of drug-resistant pneumonia in America. By 1995 up to twenty-five percent of all cases of adult pneumonia were found to be resistant to pencillin.[19] In New York, thirty percent of all cases of tuberculosis are caused by bacteria that resist antibiotics. [20]

Sadly, all this reliance on drugs does more than weaken our resistance to diseases. It also robs us of the opportunity to know God as a healer, both through divine healing and through the use of natural medicines and a healthy, God-honouring lifestyle. Christian pioneers like the Quaker leader George Fox, taught a great deal about natural healing, with God's help. John Wesley, founder of the Methodist movement, wrote *Primitive Medicine*, a book on home remedies. The world needs to see people who are basing their approach to health on Scripture and its principles rather than medical trends alone.

All truth is God's truth. Medical science certainly plays a vital role in our lives, and rightly so, as it too is a wonderful gift from God. But our *faith* should be in God first.

1. See Daniel 1:1-5
2. Deuteronomy 28:9-10
3. Deuteronomy 4:6-8
4. Revelation 17:14 (cf. 1 John 4:3)
5. 1 John 2:18
6. Genesis 11:4-9
7. Genesis 2:24
8. Matthew 22:37-39
9. For more information on Mark and Darlene's work, *Mercy Ministries, Australia* - go to: www.mercyministries.com.au or e-mail: info@mercyministries.com.au
10. UK Office of National Statistics, *Social Trends 28*, 1998.
11. *The Observer*, Dec 22, 1995
12. Ibid.
13. *Divorce Today Factsheet*, OnePlusOne pub., 1998
14. Genesis 2:24
15. Matthew 2:14
16. Matthew 28:19
17. Matthew 19:6 and Malachi 2:16
18. Winkie Pratney, *Fire on the Horizon* (Renew Books, 1999), p. 21.
19. Ibid. p. 22.
20. Ibid. p. 22.

3

Reinventing You

It's 1924. The Olympics are set for Paris. A young Scotsman is on a ship with the rest of the British team, preparing to run for his nation.

He looks back on his days as a champion rugby player; he recalls his long training runs over the hills around his highland home. He smiles at the memory of his kid sister, with her strong ideas on what he should and should not do with his life.

'You've got to give up this running,' she'd told him. 'You need to concentrate on your Christian outreach work. God has called you to be a missionary, like your father.'

He'd decided that, yes, he would become a missionary. That was his prime goal in life. Yet, he could also glorify God by excelling in athletics - and he had one race in which to do it.

Now, here he is on the deck of the ship, enjoying the camaraderie of his fellow athletes. Word reaches him that the schedule for the games has finally been posted on deck. Like everyone else, he runs to find out when he'll make his big appearance.

To his horror, his one and only race has been scheduled for a Sunday. In that moment he knows he must withdraw. There's nothing else for it. He cannot, in good conscience, run on the Lord's day.

The news spread like fire around the ship - Eric Lidell refused to run. Something to do with religious principles, they said. The speedy Scot was the acknowledged favourite to win his race. The whole of Britain felt it, and expected it.

The team coach, shocked by the news, asked him to reconsider. Eric held his ground. The Prince of Wales happened to be aboard the ship. He asked to see Liddell in his private quarters. The team leadership hoped that being asked to run by his future king would make some difference to this stubborn young man. It did not. He said his obedience to God must take precedence over obedience to men, even princes and kings.

His story was carried back to Britain, and to the world, via the major newspapers of the day. The young man who defied a king became an unwitting celebrity - to some, a villain.

Finally, a team compromise of sorts was worked out. Eric would run in a different race, one for which he had not trained. He probably wouldn't win, but who knows, he might get a place.

Eric did run that race. And, with his unique running style - head thrown back as if to suck in as much oxygen as possible - he won! His victory was a cause for national celebration, and years later a Hollywood screenwriter turned his fascinating story into a hit movie we know as *Chariots of Fire.*

Though it must have taken enormous courage to do so, especially in those bygone days when duty was everything, a young Scotsman stood up to a king. What gave him this enormous courage and tenacity? It was his sense of who he was under God. No earthly king would make his ultimate choices - he was called by a higher authority. He knew who he was - and *whose* he was.

What Should I Call You?

If you were a Hebrew living at the time of Daniel, even your name would hold a special, spiritual significance for you. It was meant to suggest something about your destiny.

Almost as soon as they landed in Babylon, Nebuchadnezzar removed the names given to Daniel and his friends at their circumcision, each of which contained the name of the Hebrew God. He replaced them with names that spoke of major Chaldean deities. For example, Daniel (God is my judge) became Belteshazzar (keeper of hidden treasures of Bel). His friend Mishael (he that is the strong God) became Meshach (of the goddess of Shach). Shach, or Venus, was part of the pantheon of Babylonian gods. [1]

Our post-modern Babylon tries to strip us of our special identity under God by getting us to call ourselves by something other than God's names for us. It's been doing this in two ways.

Firstly, people have been heavily influenced by evolutionary theory. Charles Darwin said that he never meant to kill God but, in the minds of many people, that's exactly what he did. After Darwin, people began to think that perhaps God had been just an invention to help us make sense of our world until science came along and offered us the real answers.

Before Darwin, people were able to argue that the complexity we see in the natural world is the result of its having an intelligent and creative designer. After Darwin's theories became popular, it was evolution that gave the world its complexity. God didn't create the species we see; this was a result of the process of natural selection.

There was another flow on from this: human beings themselves were no longer special creations made in God's image. We were no longer the children of God; we became descendants of apes and swamp things! Not only did God shrink in importance, so did we. Bryan Appleyard writes that man gradually came to see himself as being: 'half way between being and nothingness ... [and science thus gave us] modern man, alone, self-created, self-defining and baffled by the world.'[2]

Like it or not, after Darwin we went from being sons of God to sons of the apes, from children of the heavens to children of the algae. If we teach our children that they are merely 'monkeys who got lucky', animals with a few accidental advantages, why should we be so surprised if they start acting like animals - or worse than animals? If we teach kids that there is no ultimate arbiter of morality - and therefore, no absolute right and wrong - what's to stop them becoming anarchists who rebel against any and every system of order? If we tell people that human beings have no special destiny under God, what's to stop them giving in to despair?

Today, not even the most ardent proponent of scientific progressivism could argue that the wonderful 'New World' promised by science has actually materialised. In fact, our technology - a blessing though it so often is - has been the tool through which human beings have done incalculable harm to one another.

In one day of the 1916 Battle of the Somme, the first battle in which tanks were used, more lives were lost than in the whole of the previous century of wars in Europe. After this, two centuries of positivistic humanism, the progeny of the Enlightenment, lay buried in the muddy fields of northern France. Humanism has never fully recovered.

Later, we witnessed the horrors of Auschwitz and Berkenwald and the atom bomb made its awesome and terrifying appearance at Hiroshima. Appleyard observes that, 'the innocence of the easy, progressive Enlightenment myth ... finally died ... [We saw that] scientific reason was as capable of producing monsters as unreason ... The horror of the twentieth century revealed that the severance of knowledge and value has terrible consequences.'[3]

DIY Religion

There is another way in which Babylon has been attacking our sense of identity under God. People today are bombarded with all kinds of religious options. Nowadays, you can shop for religion as you might shop for grocery items. You can be eclectic, taking a little of this and a little of that and mixing it all together to build your own do-it-yourself, designer religion. In the end, you have a kind of faith that is purely subjective. You are no better off than you would be *without* religion. You have nothing but your own wisdom on which to build your life; no sense of moral direction other than the one your own fickle heart can provide.

The ancient Babylonians were very spiritually minded people and their ideas about religion helped to shape their whole world-view and cultural identity. The name of their city meant 'gateway to the gods' and their famous ziggurats - pyramid-like terraced temples - were actually man-made mountains that the priests would ascend in the hope of meeting with the gods.

However, the religion of Babylon was not based on God's revelation; it was a human design based on trying to make God after man's image. Their gods were gods they could control - and who allowed them to control other people. In some ways, as is often the case with false faiths, their religious system was based on perversions of scriptural truth.

The Heaven's Gate cult, the Branch Davidians and the Solar Temple group are all recent examples of cults built on the perversion of Christian teachings, and the use of religion to manipulate people.

The religious and cultural life of the Babylonians was also a strange mix of science, pseudo-science and spirituality. Today, we also see a blurring of the lines between science and spirituality. We have religions built on the idea of contact with extra-terrestrial beings that have supposedly come to us using 'advanced technology'. We have groups like the Scientologists whose teaching is a strange mix of sci-fi techno-speak and religious imagery.

In fact, in many ways, science itself has become the new religion for some people. It's not faith, but science that's become the 'opiate of the masses'. Since we were very young, most of us have been conditioned to think in a scientific way. We are taught, or encouraged, to rationalise away spiritual things, to deny the possibility of miracles (while still hoping they might happen for us) and to ignore what we can't experience with our physical senses. We have substituted hedonism for heroism and the pursuit of pleasant experiences for spiritual meaning.

Where once religious faith influenced every part of people's lives; faith in science now pervades every facet of our experience. It won't be long before we allow scientists not only to cure but also to try to *prevent* disease by playing with our very genes.

People are often lulled into a false sense of security about the future believing that technology will pull us through no matter what we face. Technology is all about utility and efficiency: it looks for faster, more economical ways of doing things. In that sense technology is completely amoral. Technology can provide solutions to practical needs, but we, the users, must make the moral choices on how, where or even *if* the technology should be used.

Today, we are facing the problem of technological growth that outstrips the pace of moral and ethical debate. We are running ahead of our capacity to weigh up the ethics and morality of new techniques. Scientists and ethicists are aware of something they call the Law of Unlimited Consequences. It states that, as nature is both complex *and* subtle, we can change things but we *cannot* predict the ramifications of the changes further down the track. For example, with the mapping of the human genome and the development of technologies based on this, how can we possibly foresee the consequences in nature in, say, one hundred years time?

'Science,' says Appleyard, 'now answers questions as if it were a religion ... But it confronts none of the spiritual issues of purpose and meaning.'[4] It is our sense of purpose, of who we are and why we're here, that ultimately shapes our morality. Science does not address those issues because it cannot. Observation and experimentation have never been and will never be enough to fully interpret the universe we live in, or our own selves. Observation can point us in the right direction, but only revelation can show us the big picture. Morality can only flourish in an atmosphere of belief in God and without a moral compass to guide us we will flounder on the rocks of our own inventiveness.

How Do You Know That?

When Babylon changed Daniel's reading habits, it was not simply giving him a new library card. It was trying to change the way in which knowledge came to him.

Education, whatever the particular discipline, is about much more than teaching facts. One dictionary defines education as: 'the process, beginning at birth, of developing intellectual capacity, natural skill and social awareness, especially by giving instruction.'

Education is about developing in someone the ability to reach his or her highest potential. It's about expanding our intelligence, which is sometimes defined as the ability to make fine distinctions. Education helps tune our ability to distinguish between ideas, to link individual concepts into an overall perception.

Education imparts a method of learning and a way of looking at things. An arts student will always look at things through a different eye than will a maths student. They will both try to learn about something in a different way, because of the different emphases used in their education. I'm very grateful for my own twelve years in school and five years in university. Those years taught me a lot, not just about certain academic disciplines, but about life and people and how to think.

Education is a major blessing. For a Christian, education is especially important. Yes, I know that many people think Christianity is all about kissing your mental faculties goodbye. That's because they confuse *faith* with *fantasy* and *innocence* with *ignorance*. The fact is that if you were committed to education *before* you became a Christian, you should probably be *much more* committed now.

First of all, education allows you and me to develop to the full our God-given, natural abilities. Some educators are now talking about there being different kinds of genius. While traditional I.Q. (intelligence quotient) tests only measured a certain type of mental ability, teachers are now recognising that there are other kinds of intelligence, which are equally important. One of the pioneers of this thinking was a man called Howard Gardner. He identified seven different kinds of intelligence:

1. Verbal-linguistic: the ability to read and write words.
2. Numerical: the ability to deal with data measured in numbers.
3. Spatial: an ability to create using three-dimensional constructs.
4. Physical: athletic or mechanical ability.
5. Intrapersonal: this is often called 'emotional intelligence' and refers to how a person deals with the emotional aspects of his or her own personality.
6. Interpersonal: the ability to relate easily to other people, to communicate.
7. Environmental: a genius for dealing with our natural surroundings.[5]

There are, some say, more than thirty major types of intelligence. The point is that different people learn best in different ways. Some people, with a high level of verbal-linguistic intelligence, will learn best from reading and writing and traditional forms of education. Others, who are have a high tendency toward 'physical intelligence', will learn more when they're involved in some kind of physical activity - playing a sport, for example.

If you're a person with a strong interpersonal kind of intelligence, you may learn better when you're communicating something to other people, in a speech for example. The way you learn will be determined by the type of intelligence you possess.

We don't need to go into more detail here. The point is that we *all* possess unique intellectual abilities. Many of these can never be measured by traditional I.Q. testing, which really only deals with a few of these types of intelligence. Even if you did not rate highly in school exams, perhaps because your ability in verbal-linguistics is low, you will still find that you are highly intelligent in other ways.

Robert T. Kiyosaki is a millionaire businessman and author of the best-selling *Rich Dad* book series. In his books, he relates how he struggled in school. He found many of the classes boring, and he constantly fell behind other kids as he battled to learn the required material. At the same time, he had no trouble at all learning about the world of finance, helped along by a friend's business-man father.

Much later, he discovered that his problem at school wasn't so much related to the subject matter, as to the method of teaching. He had low verbal-linguistic skills, which meant that he found normal classroom teaching difficult. However, he had no problem with learning through the use of diagrams and pictures. His friend's father often used diagrams of balance sheets, for example, to train him in becoming a financial success. Robert also had no problem learning if he was in some of competitive setting - playing a sport, or even a board game. He was a much better interactive learner than he was a textbook learner.

Years later, he turned these strengths to his advantage by developing, for example, a series of board games that have educated many thousands of children, teenagers and adults in financial management and entrepreneurial thinking. He became a huge success, as a businessman and as an educator, by identifying where he learned best. He recognised his particular kind of intelligence and applied himself to learn accordingly.

It is up to each of us, with the help of parents and teachers early in life, and later our friends, to discover and develop our particular strengths. These are God given and are intended to enrich our lives and bring success as we make our contribution to the world. We each need to seek out education in areas where we will learn best. That makes God famous by honouring his nature and character, both of which are expressed in our abilities.

Why Should I Believe?

Christians should also be interested in education because the secular world needs answers of substance. In this world, there are Christians who have something to say and Christians who have to say something. We should aim to position ourselves in the first category. More than ever, the world needs advocates for Christian truth who can really communicate age-old wisdom and eternal truth in a way that relates to everyday, real-world concerns. C. S. Lewis used to say that we need good philosophy if only to answer the claims of bad philosophy. What we need today are people of faith who can present positive Bible-based responses to social and lifestyle issues.

You see, the gospel of Jesus Christ doesn't start and end with one or two New Testament texts, and it's not just a spiritual message. The gospel is a total *world-view* - it's a whole way of seeing reality, of interpreting the way the world is and explaining why we're here and where we're going. What's more, it's the only world-view that *works* - the only one that lines up with the way things really are all around us.

The Christian world-view is founded upon four major concepts: Creation, Fall, Redemption and Restoration. We were created in the image of God.[6] We fell from grace.[7] God made a way to buy us back for himself, to pay the death penalty for sin.[8] Through Christ, we can be restored to the place of favour God intended for us.[9]

Why is the Christian church not reaching the masses, as we'd like it to? Why do so many people hear our message and then pass on by with scarcely a second look? It's often because we don't engage people where they are most *ready* to be challenged and most *susceptible* to change - in the realm of ideas. Ideas shape our entire lives. We all behave according to our world-view; our picture of what is real and important.

Most people today wouldn't know what 'post-modernism' means, yet they live as post-modernists. Post-modernism started as a movement in arts and architecture, then it spread to philosophy and now, decades later, it has come to affect the thoughts and actions of millions of people. Modernism in design arts taught that technique was more important than form. 'Who cares about decoration?' it said. 'What matters is function.' Individual style wasn't important, so it tried to reduce every new design to a few basic standards.

Post-modernism was a reaction against that. It said that life's about more than doing a job and meeting a need; it's about beauty and experience as well. It rejected the idea that one style could fit all. All styles are equally valid, it said. Applying this thinking to morality and ethics, people then started saying, 'There is no absolute moral right or wrong. All *moral* points of view are correct, all *life*styles are equally valid.'

This kind of thinking is rampant in our culture today. People don't first seek truth; they look for 'meaningful experiences'. Tolerance used to mean, 'You can do that if you want, but it's wrong.' Now, it means, 'You can do that if you want because *nothing* is wrong.' Post-modernism is a world-view, a way of seeing reality, a basis for people's choices and behaviour.

It's a world-view that is aeons away from that of the Bible. Yet, many Christian leaders behave as if all we have to do is quote John 3:16 and people will yield their will to Christ. Some others behave as if all people need is a 'power encounter', in a revival meeting. Many people who do have a power encounter simply file it away with all their other 'positive, mystical experiences' - like their recent tarot reading, or the 'meaningful sex' they had last week.

Unless we start meeting the world head-on in the world of ideas, we'll forever live in a bunker; scared to engage real people for fear that we won't have answers to the big questions. And the only Christians pagan post-moderns will meet will be those who have lost touch with reality, who live in a fairy land of meaningless cliches and pat answers. Or Christians who lead almost the same life they do, with pretty much the same goals - health, happiness and financial upward mobility.

There is no need for Christians to feel intimidated or overwhelmed whenever the word 'ideas' is mentioned. When Paul faced the Athenians in Acts 17, he didn't need to confront them with heavy philosophy. He simply showed them that their view of reality couldn't compete with that of the Bible! He saw that there were gaping holes in their view of the world and themselves - holes even they recognised. There were a lot of things they just couldn't get to add up in their philosophy, and so they'd erected their statue to an 'unknown god'.

Paul filled in the blanks, confronting them with the truth that was missing. Paul didn't need to resort to any heavy philosophy, he just told the gospel story - from the beginning, and starting in the realm of ideas. Some of them came to faith in Christ that day.[10]

Who knows what impact these thinkers went on to make with their newfound faith? We can do the same in our times and with similar results! Think about it: who else but a Christian is telling people that they're not the chance result of evolution, but created beings - and created for greatness?

Who else is preaching that people are not basically good, but fallen from grace - a fact most people feel intuitively?

Who else is telling people that they can't find redemption and grace through money, or sex, or success? And who else is able to say that there *is* hope in this sin-bruised universe, because Christ is at the end of our story just as he is at the beginning?

Creation, Fall, Redemption, and Restoration: it's a story that worked with pagan Athenians. It's worked for me hundreds of times when I've been speaking to crowds in college auditoriums, secular nightclubs and others non-religious venues. With God's help, it will work for you. Take every opportunity to tell people that *whole* story. The wholeness of that gospel world-view, the fact that it *does* match reality, makes God famous.

Have Influence, Or Be Influenced!

One writer called knowledge, 'the frontier of tomorrow'. Another said that, 'the future belongs to those who plan for it.' Others have said that we are now living in the knowledge society, where the educated are the true capitalists and the new currency is information. Knowledge is money - and influence.

The word 'influence' simply refers to the ability to bring change. Every one of us was born for influence! You were not born to be overlooked, which is why being ignored feels so painful. When you came to Christ, you received the power of God's Holy Spirit to make some radical changes to our world. You were called to challenge the status quo and to point the way to something better - the Kingdom of God. You're destined to be part of a church that is like a city set on a hill. It cannot be hidden - or ignored.[11]

The battle between the flesh and the spirit is a battle of influence. The tussle between light and darkness is a struggle for influence. Here's the bottom line: if you don't influence your world, your world will most certainly influence you! Most people don't come into influence by accident: it is a matter of choice, preparation and forethought. Do you want to be a person of influence? Do you want to change your environment more than it changes you? Then you must prepare for long-term influence today.

If knowledge is the new currency of our age, if techniques and information are the keys to bringing change to our world, then we should be educating ourselves toward that end. Notice what Paul says in Romans:

> 'Do not conform any longer to the pattern of this world, but be transformed by the renewing of your mind. Then you will be able to test and approve what God's will is - his good, pleasing and perfect will.' (Romans 12:2)

He does not say we're transformed by the *removing* of our minds. The mind has to be *renewed* through cooperation with the Holy Spirit. The word used here means to renovate, as you would refit a house. The Holy Spirit wants to help me pull down some of the old, musty and darkened rooms in the house of my mind. These are rooms that have held nothing but trunk loads of painful memories, inferiority and rejection. He wants to knock through some walls, creating new windows and doors. He wants to shine light into shadowy areas, opening my mind to new vistas and horizons.

If that's what the Holy Spirit is all about, a Christian ought to be more thoughtful and clear-thinking than is any other person.

There's one other thing I need to say here. All of the above factors should motivate us to develop our minds, but the *major* reason to do so is this: Jesus said that honouring God with the mind is the part of the greatest of all commandments. He said we should love God with all our heart (spirit and will), soul (emotions and feelings), mind (intellect and rational thought) and strength (physical body and energy).[12] Whether you're a Rhodes scholar, or someone who has never had much formal schooling; whether you're a genius with numbers or at your best with physical activities; whatever way you learn best, you can develop your mental abilities to the max, out of love for God. You can prepare for influence, to make God famous.

1. Every one of the Jewish names for these men contained God's name in the form of *El* or *Jah.* Daniel (God is my judge) became Belteshazzar (keeper of hidden treasures of Bel). Hananiah (The grace of the Lord) became Shadrach (the inspiration of the sun). The sun was worshipped by the Chaldeans. Mishael (He that is the strong God) became Meshach (of the goddess of Shach). Shach, or Venus, was a god in Babylonians. Azariah (The Lord is a help) became Abed-nego (the servant of the shining fire). The Caledonia people worshipped fire.
2. Bryan Appleyard, *Understanding the Present* (Picador, 1992, 93) pp.58-59
3. Ibid., pp.122 and 139
4. Ibid., p.228
5. For more on this subject, see *Rich Kid Smart Kid* by Robert T. Kiyosaki (TechPress, 2001)
6. Genesis 1:26-27
7. Romans 3:23
8. Galatians 3:14
9. Romans 6:23
10. Acts 17:22-34
11. Matthew 5:14
12. See Mark 12:30

4

Revelation Man

I'm speaking at an event in the north of England. There's a call on my mobile phone. It's a friend of mine called Stuart Bell. He's a nationally respected Christian leader who heads a significant church in the old city of Lincoln, and a network of churches across the country. He wants me to get down to his place as soon as possible.

'What's the hurry?' I ask.

'There's a prophetess visiting my church. She says she has a personal message from God for you. I think you should get down here tonight.'

Now, I've been around the church all my life and I've seen many a so-called prophet come and go. I've heard all the flakes, so I'm a little cautious. But I trust Stuart, because he's been around too!

'I know you wouldn't call if you didn't think was important, but I've got to speak tonight,' I tell him. 'Besides, getting to you will take a couple of hours drive, at least.'

Stuart is insistent.

'I'll tell your driver I need you here straight after your meeting. There'll be no problem. I really think you should meet this woman. She's from the USA and, though she's never met you or heard of you, she woke up this morning with your name in her mind. She described to me the kind of work you do as if she knew you well, and then she told me God has given her this message for you, which she must deliver in person! '

By now, I have to be honest, I'm becoming more than a little curious. So, after preaching my heart out, and feeling ready for bed, I find myself jumping in a car for the long drive to the Lincoln. When we finally arrive, a little the worse for wear, we make our way into the rear of the church, where a meeting is still in progress.

Eventually, my friend calls me to the front and introduces me to the woman who is ministering. As soon as she opens her mouth, it's as if she's been reading my mail. Now, I guess I've given thousands of personal prophetic messages for people in my own ministry through the years. But when you're on the receiving end, well, it's freaky, exhilarating and sobering all at the same time - especially when someone is being as specific as this woman is.

Later, as I walk away from the meeting, I know God has given me some major encouragement about our work in Europe. And there's one thing for sure - he's really inspired me to take more risks to make him famous.

I don't need to relate what that woman said to me, but when I left that night, I had a lot to think about, and a lot to thank God for. I had some things confirmed for me and learned some very important things - about my situation, my future and my God! Of course, I would never base my actions on one word of prophecy alone, but I could not have gained that kind of very specific, personalised information from a book or an adult college course. No amount of education could possible have given me the encouragement, inspiration or specific insight that one *revelation message* provided.

Education Without Revelation

You see, as important as education is, we were never designed to learn through education alone who we are and what is our place in the world. When God created us, he meant us to learn in more than one way, on more than one level. Yes, he built into our make-up the thirst to understand the natural world around us, and the capacity to use observation, logic and reason to explain what we see. That's what we develop through different kinds of education, from scholastic work to sports training. But God also invested in us an even more precious gift: the ability to seek knowledge that is beyond our natural senses. He gave us the capacity to learn by revelation, to learn through faith.

Revelation is higher than education because its *object* is higher: learning about God. If we are truly made in God's image, if he does have a special purpose for our lives, then nothing can be more important than discovering what he is like and what he wants for us. Herbert Spencer, an agnostic, said that if human beings were to know anything about God, he would need to reveal himself to them. That's exactly what the Bible says God has done. He has shown something of himself in his creation,[1] in the Scriptures,[2] and, ultimately, in his Son.[3]

Joan Osborne asked a great question with her song *What if God was One of Us?*. I'd like to meet Joan; I'd like to tell her that her question has already been answered. At a specific time in history, God put on human form as we might put on an overcoat. He came in a form we can understand. He heard the cry of our heart for revelation and said, 'This is what I'm like.'

In today's world, however, many people are robbed of the chance to discover God. They are offered education without revelation. This gives rise to a society which is built on technology without truth.

The major claim to acceptance of any new technology is that 'it works'. Technological development is based on pragmatism, on getting practical results. We buy into new technologies because they give us helpful new techniques for doing everyday things. Traditionally, technologies came into existence in response to human need. Tools existed because we needed them. We accepted new technologies because they clearly made our lives better. In our time, though, many new techniques exist *only because* the technology is there to make them possible. In other words, the technology often runs ahead of our ability to decide if it is helpful or not!

In many cases, there is very little discussion about where technology is taking us over all, or about what specific technologies might mean to our basic humanity or our environment. At the moment, for example, there are not too many people who think that human cloning would be a good idea, but few people foresee a time when it will not be happening at some level.

Technology thrives on pragmatism and that's fine, up to a point. We generally love it when we find gadgets that will do things better, faster and more economically. Yet pragmatism on its own can sometimes work against truth. The Bible puts it like this:

'There is a way that seems right to a man, but in the end it leads to death.' (Proverbs 14:12)

Sometimes a man-made solution to a problem may seem to work, but it may lead to spiritual and even physical ruin down the track. Only *revelation* can provide the objective bedrock on which we can base healthy debates on the moral implications of technologies like cloning or gene therapy.

In the natural world, the principle of entropy says that any natural system left to itself, without any outside energy source, tends to wind down. If I take a jug of water and plug it into an electric socket and turn it on, it will gradually come to the boil. Once I turn off the power, though, it quickly cools again. Its energy winds down.

It's the same with us on a spiritual or moral level. Without a constant input of revelation, of truth that is based on God's character, we tend to sink toward the lowest common denominator. Without revelation, we will go on making the same mistakes as we have always made. Only as time goes by and our technological power grows, we will make those mistakes on an even bigger scale. Revelation does not work against technology; it helps us keep technology in check. It helps us ensure that technology remains our servant and never becomes our master.

Overcoming Babylon - With A Truth That Is 'Out There'

Here's the remarkable thing about Daniel. Despite the incredible repression he experienced, the challenge to his identity and the pressure to conform, he remained a man of godly faith throughout his life. His adverse surroundings did not change his inner commitment to God!

Some Christians are filled with optimism when their circumstances allow. When things start going a little sour, however, or when people or events don't match up to their expectations, they start flinging the mud of criticism or recrimination. They start doubting God and blaming others, instead of standing their ground in faith, as the Bible says we can.[4]

Daniel not only *survived* in Babylon - he overcame its influence! He actually outlived five kings of that city - and he *outshone* them in his life of moral principle and excellence. Throughout history, most people would never have heard of kings like Nebuchadnezzar, had it not been for their connection with the life of Daniel. He was kidnapped in his youth and sold as a slave. Yet, like another slave-boy called Patricius, whom we call St. Patrick, Daniel rose above his cruel circumstances to bring a unique message from God at a turning point in history. Like Patrick, whose influence later saved western civilisation from the ruinous barbarians, Daniel went on to make a great name for his God. In so doing, he also cemented his own place in history. How did Daniel achieve this level of influence? What was his secret?

Above all else, Daniel is known in the Bible as a man of revelation. He had an extraordinary capacity for hearing from God. He could read the secret dreams of kings and see visions of future events. This is what set him apart in Babylon, right from the start.[5] This is what turned the hearts of pagan rulers.[6] It is what gave Daniel his longevity, causing him to outlast his enemies.[7] And, above all else, his hunger for revelation is what gave Daniel great favour with God.[8]

Perhaps the single most defining moment in the life of Daniel is his prophecy of the downfall of Babylon. Often, prophecies are given and then remain unfulfilled for many years - sometimes for generations. In this case, Daniel's words became reality in just one night.[9]

King Belshazzar's party - *orgy* might be a more accurate word for it - was in full swing. The guests were gyrating to whatever type of music they were into back then. Drugs were in fast supply and the alcohol was flowing fast. Suddenly, much to the consternation, the horror, of the distinguished guests, a huge hand began to write on the tiled centre wall of the banqueting chamber. What made it all really spooky was that the hand was not in any way attached to anything. There was no arm, no body.

When the invisible graffiti artist was done, they found four words scribbled across the wall, in laser print. Belshazzar and his friends could read the words - that much was not difficult. The words were simple: *mene* (or *mina*, a small number or unit of money), *tekel* (another word for *shekel*, a unit of weight) and *parson* (a half-shekel or half-mina). The first word was repeated twice, for emphasis.[10]

To the partygoers, these words didn't seem related at all, so the message didn't make any sense. Everyone was in a real flap until one of the assembled crew remembered talk of a man who could understand mysteries and decipher visions. So, though Daniel was no longer part of the king's inner court, he was brought out of retirement.

Daniel was the only one who could read the writing on the wall. He alone could take the four seemingly unrelated words and put them together to show what God was saying to his generation:

'This is what these words mean: Mene: God has numbered the days of your reign and brought it to an end. Tekel: You have been weighed on the scales and found wanting. Peres: Your kingdom is divided and given to the Medes and Persians.' (Daniel 5:26-28)

People in our times know that, in many ways, 'the writing is on the wall.' All around them they see danger signs on the road ahead. Ask any group of students today, 'What are the things that concern you most?' You'll get answers like 'environmental catastrophe', 'global warming', 'nuclear disaster', 'ozone depletion', 'ethnic unrest', 'violence' and so on. These are like the words hand-written on Belshazzar's wall.

Anyone can see the individual problems, but few can see the big picture and see the impact overall. Even fewer can see where *God* is in all this, or where we are in his timetable, or what he might be calling us to do. A. W. Tozer left us with these insightful words to think about:

'The prophet is one who knows his times and what God is trying to say to the people of his times... Today we need prophetic preachers; not preachers of prophecy but preachers with a gift of prophecy... It is not the ability to predict that we need, but the anointed eye, the power of spiritual penetration and interpretation, the ability to appraise the religious scene as viewed from God's perspective and to tell us what is actually going on.'

'What is needed desperately today is prophetic insight. Scholars can interpret the past; it takes prophets to interpret the present. Learning will enable a man to pass judgement on our yesterdays; but it requires a gift of clear seeing to pass sentence on our own day. One hundred years from now, historians will know what was taking place religiously in this year of our Lord; but that will be too late for us. We need to know right now.'[11]

In a sense, every Christian is prophetic and every Christian is a preacher. The role of the prophetic voice is summed up for us in the word God gave to Jeremiah:

'Then the LORD reached out his hand and touched my mouth and said to me, "Now, I have put my words in your mouth. See, today I appoint you over nations and kingdoms to uproot and tear down, to destroy and overthrow, to build and to plant."' (Jer 1:9-10)

A truly prophetic life is one that challenges the status quo and points the way to something higher, something better. It calls a generation, a people or a nation to line up with God's agenda, while revealing what that agenda might be.

The generations we are serving need people like Daniel who are able to read the writing on the wall, who can read between the lines, guided by the Holy Spirit. In this age, we are waiting to hear prophetic voices raised to declare, 'Thus says the Lord.' We are in desperate need of forward thinkers who can marry revelation vision to revelation strategy, and thus bring about real-world change.

Hi-Tech, Hi-Need

There are three distinct generations that make up the major part of western society today: the so-called Baby Boomers (aged 40s to 60s), Generation X (aged 20s to late 30s) and Generation Y, or the Millenials (aged late teens and under). Each generation is unique and has different needs. (That's the subject for a later book in this series.) Yet they all have one thing in common. They are all hungry for revelation - though, often, they don't know it.

There's no doubt, modern technology has given us a great deal. Early on, industrial technology gave us the ability to produce more. In the 1800s, one farmer could produce enough food for about four people. With machinery and fertilizers, one farmer can now produce enough food for about one hundred people. Industrial technology increased our leisure time - in the 1800s, people worked for twelve to sixteen hour days, with no paid holidays - and gave many of us a much higher standard of living.

Today, information technology has added a whole new dimension to many daily tasks and experiences. It took radio thirty-eight years to attract fifty million listeners. It took television thirteen years to attract the same number of viewers. It took just four year for the ubiquitous Internet to draw in its first fifty million users. This technology alone is dramatically changing the way we buy and sell and even the way we form relationships. We've already seen amazing things, but information technology is still only taking its first baby steps.

With the advance of technology, though, we all know there have also been some less desirable effects. Environmental pollution and the depletion of natural resources, for example. Fossil fuels are being used up at a rapid rate and freeways, factories and junkyards clutter up the landscape. Technology has helped many industries expand, offering new jobs to workers. At the same time, though, machines have taken many jobs away, shifting the focus from manual or technical work to mental work.

Perhaps one of the most powerful results of the boom in technology has been the growing sense of alienation it has brought for many people. Some psychologists and sociologists are now talking about a new phenomenon they call 'technological alienation'. The word 'alienation' simply means a sense of powerlessness and estrangement. Sometimes, when we feel overwhelmed by the rapid changes around us, when we experience what Alvin Toffler called 'future shock', we have feelings of apathy or resignation and of being cut off from fellow human beings. In the face of all the new choices facing us, we may find ourselves saying: 'I can't change anything, so why bother getting involved in the first place? Why bother being passionate about anything?'

The rapid growth in our reliance on technology does sometimes contribute to alienation between people groups. It boosts the advantage one group has over another. In Europe and North American today, well over one hundred million people regularly use the Internet. But in Africa, just a few million people have access to that technology. In America, you might save for one month to buy a new PC, but in Bangladesh it will take you eight years. Even *within* developed countries, there are many invisible 'technology ghettoes' - whole communities where the benefits of the information explosion are never felt because people don't have access to new technology. If knowledge and information are the currency of the new age, and you can't access them, you're never able to pull yourself out of the cycle of poverty. That can also lead to racial problems because the line between the have's and the have not's in many communities is also a line between the races.

Technology can also alienate people from social structures. Many people today feel isolated from or cynical about their governments and public institutions, not to mention big corporations. Technology has contributed to that mistrust, especially in the area of privacy invasion, for many people the most dangerous corollary of the modern technological age.

When we think of privacy invasion, some of us see sinister images of illegal phone taps or hidden surveillance cameras - or TV cameras from *Big Brother*. But the real threat to our privacy is much more mundane and close to home. Every day, we buy, sell and move money around in ways that are recorded by electronic machines. That information is shuffled around by companies and institutions, until we can't really control *who* knows *what* about *us*. Large companies are hiring other companies to gather information on the buying habits of individual consumers. Companies are even using electronic surveillance systems on their own workers: to monitor their telephone conversations, e-mails and time on the Internet. Big brother has become 'big boss'.

Governments and public institutions have also become more intrusive. Public service bodies have grown enormously in recent times not because of population growth so much as the great increase in the amount of data they collect and analyse. The reasons they give for this can be quite legitimate - for example, to provide better health services or to fight crime. In major Western countries, police are compiling national DNA databases of convicted criminals. This may be a good idea in some ways, but we do pay a price. It will inevitably lead to more government surveillance of our daily lives.

On a more mundane level, our PCs, WAP phones and PDAs send an inbuilt ID code whenever we log onto the Internet. Companies can use that to track your interests. Just switching a mobile phone on means that phone companies can pretty much track our whereabouts. And the new science of biometrics is making it possible for you to be identified by your voice, your eyes, or almost any other part of your anatomy. One day, things like driver's licences, passports and credit cards might be made redundant by body-scanners.

Some consumer and civil rights groups are already warning that, in twenty years time, if we're not careful, we might have no privacy left to protect.

Beyond Those X-Files ...

In some ways, there's an even more dangerous kind of alienation than these. It's a sense of alienation from ourselves. What we are facing today is, in many ways, a battle between our technology and our humanity. There's a tug of war going on between what we feel in conscience to be right and what is made possible by modern science.

Jaques Ellul was a professor at the University of Bordeaux. He wrote 40 books and hundreds of articles, most of them dealing with what he called the threat to human faith and freedom created by modern technology. He talked about the tyranny of technology over humanity.

Ellul said that technology has taken over from Christian faith as the most sacred thing in our western society. The Christian faith is one that has ennobled the human race and given rise to the most prosperous, and civilized societies of all time. Once we couldn't live without God, said Ellul, but today we can't live without gadgets.

We've invited technology into our workplaces, then into our homes, and now even into our bodies. Before long, medico's will be able to inject tiny robots into your blood stream, to help heal you of your ailments. Many of people today live as if they take it for granted that our technology can, at least in time, meet all our most important needs. But can it?

What was it the *X-Files* told us? 'The truth is out there.' Human hearts resonate with that idea - that there is a truth beyond the realm of science, beyond what our senses alone can tell us. The younger generations, in particular, do not accept what some of their grandparents did, that all of reality can be - or one day will be - understood and measured by science. They know that there is more to real life than meets the natural eye.

Kurt Cobaine of *Nirvana* fame was considered by many to be a rock legend. He once said, 'I need to take drugs just to numb the pain.' Materially, he had access to more than he could ever need; yet his soul craved more. Shortly after making that statement, at the zenith of his moneymaking and creative powers, he took his own life.

Science and technology can give us smart cards, smart houses and even smart cars and, soon, digitised roads. Capitalism and a consumer economy can deliver material prosperity and a supply and demand lifestyle. But none of this can feed the hunger that lies deep within each one of us - the need for the transcendent.

The Matrix Has You, Neo...

The hero of the movie *The Matrix* is a guy called Neo. To the casual observer, Neo is just another bored journeyman who spends his days just going through motions, working at a boring job. At night, though, he inhabits a different cosmos. He turns on his computer and fills his hours searching for something - he's not exactly sure what it is, but he knows it's important. Neo is driven by a gnawing feeling that there's something very wrong with the world he lives in; that there's a life that's being hidden from him. He's heard about a thing called the Matrix, a computer program that's ruling peoples' lives, but which most people know nothing about. The movie tracks his quest to break out of the Matrix and find real life.

I meet thousands of Neo's all over the world: people who feel there's something missing in their world. Something deep in their psyche tells them that they were born to walk under an open heaven, to feel blessed. In reality, though, their lives seem more cursed than blessed. Some of them spend Wednesday nights watching *Lotto* on TV, waiting for their lucky numbers to come; hoping for that one big windfall that will instantly and dramatically change their quality of life. They know intuitively that there's a better life out there somewhere.

Whether we like to admit it or not, the rampant materialism and hedonism of our age will never really satisfy our deepest longings, for these are spiritual. The old preacher who wrote the book of Ecclesiastes told us why:

'[God] has also set eternity in the hearts of men...'
(Ecclesiastes 3:11)

Our hunger for spiritual meaning and reality has shown up repeatedly in our music - from Osborne's *What if God was One of Us?* to Cliff Richard's *Millennium Prayer*. When *DC Talk* released their *Supernatural* track a few years back, it went straight to number four in the U.S. charts. It said:

'Beyond this physical terrain
There's an invisible domain
Where angels battle over souls in vast array;
But down on earth is where I am,
No wings to fly, no place to stand;
Here on my knees I am a stranger in this land.'
Our movies have carried the same theme. When

George Lucas was asked why he wanted to make the second series of *Star Wars* movies, he reportedly said, 'To make people think about God.' In the original movies, biblical themes like sin, salvation and judgement turned up in sci-fi dress. With the first of the so-called 'prequels', there is even a Lucas version of the Immaculate Conception. Again, the whole theme is salvation from the tyranny of evil - and the coming of a long-awaited and prophetically anticipated saviour.

In the advertising trailers for the hit animation feature *Prince of Egypt*, the producers asked us - dared us - to 'Believe in miracles'. That classic sci-fi fairy-tale, *ET* featured a being that came down from above. He was innocent and kind and children loved him. He had powers far beyond those of human beings: he could heal a wound with just the touch of his finger. And he was raised from the dead. For anyone who has read the gospels, there's something very familiar about all of that!

As you'd expect, this hunger for spiritual reality is also reflected in the growth of world religions. Many Jews, for example, are returning to a very literal interpretation of their Scriptures, including a belief in the imminent appearance of their Messiah. On the Muslim front, there are now three million followers of Islam in the United States alone - that's more than the total membership of the Episcopalian church. Yet none of the major religious groups can match the global growth of the Christian church. Figures show conclusively, for example, that the charismatic wing of the church worldwide recently tripled in size in just twenty years.

People are hungry for spiritual reality - and they're less embarrassed to show it than ever. The writer of Deuteronomy expressed what we all feel intuitively:

> *'Man shall not live by bread alone, but by every word which proceeds from the mouth of God.'*
> *(Deuteronomy 8:3)*

Human beings were not designed to live solely on material things. We feed the body with physical food, and the soul with earthly sensations, but we were created to feed at a deeper level too, at the level of the spirit. The food we need for the spirit is revelation.

One day, Jesus' disciples expressed concern that he hadn't eaten anything for a while. He told them he had a food supply they knew nothing about. They couldn't figure out where this secret stash might be. So, he told them what he really meant:

> "'My food,' said Jesus, "is to do the will of him who sent me and to finish his work.'" (John 4:34)

Jesus fed his spirit on a constant diet of revelation. We process physical food through digestion. We process spiritual food, revelation, through obedience.

I sometimes wonder if Kurt Cobaine had ever read those words in Deuteronomy 8:3. He certainly knew, from experience, the truth of the first part of the verse. Material things alone cannot satisfy the yearnings of the soul. Sadly, he didn't live to experience the second part of the verse - the satisfaction that comes from living in revelation.

Photographs Of God

In the late 1940s, a group of sci-fi writers met to discuss what form a modern religion might take. After the meeting, most of the writers went home and probably forgot about the whole thing. One of them, however, actually did something with what he'd heard.

L. Ron Hubbard went on to found the Church of Scientology, the teachings of which feature a strange mix of psychotherapy with outer space philosophy. Scientology teaches that every human body is inhabited by a spiritual immortal called a 'Thetan'. Supposedly, Thetans are constantly being dropped to earth by flying saucers that have come from wars in the 'Galactic Federation'. Scientology, with its 'Dianetics' and its skilful and passionate - many say, ruthless - leadership, is a powerful mix of religion & pure science fiction mythmaking.

Yet, despite its strange philosophies and its questionable pseudo-scientific personal development programs, it continues to draw people from the middle classes and from the top echelons of the movie world. Why do intelligent people allow themselves to be drawn in by ideas like those of Mr. Hubbard and his followers? I could suggest a number of reasons, but one has special relevance to Christians. Often, people are attracted to these teachings and others like them, because they want a spiritual experience rather than a dogma. They want to believe in a supernatural realm that is there to help them to live to their potential.

If I showed you a photo of my wife and family you might say, 'What a great looking family!' (I hope you would!) But you could never come to know my family through a photograph. A photograph is just a two-dimensional representation of the real thing. It's just an image frozen in the past. If you're ever going to know my family, you need a here-and-now, three-dimensional manifestation - an encounter with the real people.

For a long time, parts of the Christian church have given people nothing but 'photographs of God'. All they've shown people are two-dimensional representations of God based on their particular church tradition or ritual. People have been offered images of how God looked 'once-upon-a-time'; back in the glory days of a denomination or ministry.

People around the world are screaming for an experience of the *real thing*! They want to see who God is *now* - what he would do in *their* situation; what he looks like if he is 'one of us'. How do we become Daniel's for our time? How do we bring revelation, a manifestation of God's power and wisdom, for *now* situations?

1. Romans 1:20
2. 2 Timothy 3:16
3. Colossians 1:15
4. Ephesians 6:13
5. Daniel 2:28, 47
6. Daniel 4:1-3; 8-9
7. Daniel 5:29-30; 6:1
8. Daniel 10:12
9. Daniel 5:30-31
10. Daniel 5:25-28
11. Quoted by Winkie Pratney,
    Fire on the Horizon, (Renew, 1999), p.54.

5

To See What Isn't Seen

It's April 14, 2000. A newborn baby boy named Gabriel lies sleeping in a hospital in Norway. He weighs less than three kilos, but seems to be strong and healthy. His parents are overjoyed.

Then, five days after his birth, they hear some disturbing news. Some time during the birth process or before, Gabriel had suffered a stroke, a seeping or leaking of blood on the brain. As a result, he is starting to have epileptic cramps on the right side of his body.

Little Gabriel's parents are Christian ministers. His father, Joshua Blessitt, spends many days each year carrying a cross around Norway and other parts of the world, preaching and sharing the love of Jesus with people in the street. They're first-time parents, so the news is especially frightening.

The doctors tell them that their son will have major brain damage and that he might need years of rehabilitation before he can use the right side of his body. He will experience difficulty in learning basic life skills like eating, speaking, making eye contact with others, and so on. The doctors are speaking honestly, sharing what they believe to be the truth of the situation.

Joshua feels destroyed. He tries to be strong, but pain and heaviness tear at his heart. He has no answers and no strength. He goes outside and cries. In deep anguish of soul he asks God why this has happened and what can be done.

After a few minutes, he hears a strong but small voice speaking deep in his soul: 'Whose report will you believe?' Without thinking, he responds with passion: 'We will believe the report of the Lord!'

Joshua later related to me how he went home that night and asked his home church meeting to pray for his son. At 10 PM, he arrived back at the hospital to find his wife glowing with joy. For the past hour, she said, she had been praying and felt what she described as a fire moving through her arms.

The Lord told her to lay one hand on Gabriel's chest and the other on his head. For one hour she experienced the healing power of God moving through her into her little boy - so much so that she felt as if the very bones of Gabriel's skull were moving beneath her hand. From that hour on, she was glowing with confidence that God had healed her Gabriel.

Looking back one year later, Joshua wrote these words:

'God has healed Gabriel and now he is over one year old. He is totally normal. The doctors have tried to find something wrong with Gabriel, but since that Tuesday night, not one cramp, nor any sign or symptom of brain damage has been found. The impossible became possible. The doctor's report changed to God's report.'

'I believe that Gabriel will never need to doubt God's existence, because he will know that he experienced it first hand. Think of growing up and *knowing* that God *knows* you from a young age. My wife and I give all glory to God. We know and have experienced that no other report can stand up against the report that God has for us.'

It's true! I've heard it and seen it many times myself. When God speaks, seemingly impossible situations change for the better. Joshua and his wife received revelation from God. Both of them heard from God, in different ways, that he was going to heal their son. They knew it was a certainty before it happened.

All revelation is a reflection of what God is like and in that sense, it makes God famous. In this story, God revealed that he is a Healer, a compassionate Father, and the One who knows the beginning from the end of every story. He is concerned for every individual who loves him. Can you imagine what an impact it will have as more and more Christians learn to believe for and receive the kind of revelation that heals sick bodies and opens the secrets of people's hearts?

How can we become candidates for that kind of revelation - for our situation, for the needs of others, and for the generations we serve?

A Heart After God

The greatest gift any of us can have is our love for God - and a desire to know him and his ways. God, speaking through the prophet Jeremiah, gave it to us straight:

> '... Let him who boasts boast about this: that he understands and knows me, that I am the LORD.' (Jer. 9:24)

Often, we ask God for some revelation on a specific problem or need, but we miss something very important. The first thing God will reveal is *himself!* Genesis 17:1-2 says:

> 'When Abram was ninety-nine years old, the LORD appeared to him and said, "I am God Almighty [El Shaddai]; walk before me and be blameless. I will confirm my covenant between me and you and will greatly increase your numbers."'

God gave Abram a mind-blowing promise: he and his wife would have a son, when they were well past their procreative 'use by date'. But before he did so, he first showed Abram his 'business card'. It said, 'El Shaddai, the All-Sufficient One; he who can do anything!'

This was actually the first time in human history that God had called himself by that name - and whenever God does something for the first time you can bet it's for a good reason. So, why did God choose this particular moment to call himself by this great new name? Because of the promise he was about to make. Think about it: if I came to you and said, 'I'm going to give you one million dollars', you'd say something like, 'Thanks very much' - and then snicker behind your hand. If you know me, you're aware that I don't have a million dollars to give you. If Bill Gates made the same promise, though, you'd say, 'God bless you Mr. Gates - I promise to buy more Microsoft in future!' The promise is the same in both cases - but the person making it is different. One person is equipped to *deliver* on the promise, the other is not.

God wanted Abram to know that the incredible, over-the-top, out-of-the-question promise he was about to make *would* be fulfilled because God is *El Shaddai*, the One who can do anything.

The Danish philosopher Søren Kirkegaard talked about the difference between what he called 'objective' and 'subjective revelation'. Often, we come to God looking only for objective revelation - we want the answer to some problem in point form, steps one-to-four. We want a logical, sequential construct to define what is true in a certain situation. God, however, wants first to give us *subjective* revelation. No, I don't mean subjective in the sense that it changes according to the person involved. Nothing God reveals to us at a personal level will ever contradict the general revelation he has given in his word. I mean that God wants us to know *him*, to experience *him* first. The truth about our situation or need, the answer to our problem, can only be found through knowing him, in a very personal way. He is 'the Way, the Truth, the Life'.[1] It's out of our relationship with him that comes the revelation of truth we need to carry us through.

Pontius Pilate asked Jesus what to some people might think is a really impressive question: 'What is truth?'[2] He wanted Jesus to tell him the truth about life, in bullet point form. He wanted objective truth. Sadly though, he wasn't open to subjective revelation - he didn't want *relationship* with the One who *is* the Truth.

Had he really reached out to Jesus, opening his heart to the Lord, he could have received the answers to his questions.

Learning God's Values

A few years ago, when God called Davina and me to leave Australia for Europe, we were presented with a whole series of questions. Where would we live? Where would our children go to school? How would we finance the family's costs? How would we pay for the international mission God had called us to establish, with all the international projects he was calling us to launch? How would people in Europe respond to us?

We had spent over fifteen years building up a large ministry in Australia. We had been at the forefront of perhaps the greatest move of God's Spirit among young people in our nation's history. It was an awesome privilege to be the first national leader of a great pioneer movement like Youth Alive Australia. It was a phenomenal blessing to work with one the greatest leadership teams I have ever seen anywhere in the world! The key members of that team are now the leaders of the fastest growing, most creative churches and ministries in my homeland.

Along the way, hundreds of leaders and pastors had been raised up through the work of Youth Alive. Personally, God had given us great favour and we were able to develop a very good reputation in the ministry across our nation, and beyond. To this day, the Youth Alive model is inspiring outreach and church growth across the world.

You can imagine that, when God first called me away from this, I spent many agonising hours praying on what might lay ahead. After all, how do you follow something that had grown from just three hundred young people in one city, to over sixty thousand across a nation, in its first ten years? (It's much bigger now!)

At the time God called us to Western Europe, there were no other Australians doing what God had called us to do, on the scale we felt he wanted us to do it. The structure of our denomination's missions program was not big enough to facilitate what God was laying in my heart, though it has changed since then! During that period of waiting on God, we felt fairly lonely much of the time. So, there were many pressing practical questions for which I needed answers. I prayed hard, yet the answers I wanted didn't come in the ways I'd been expecting.

At one point, I was asking God about money - something we all need if we're to live and fulfil the call of God on our lives. Europe is not cheap and the often heavy-handed, high-tax, high-control bureaucracies of the social democrat nations are hard to deal with if, like us, you're from the 'New World'. We were selling everything we had to transplant a family of five to the 'uttermost part of the earth'. How would we finance it all?

How did God respond? He challenged me on something that didn't seem at all related to the questions I'd been asking. A good friend of mine, a respected Christian leader in our city of Melbourne, had asked me if I would carry his resume with me on our 1994 family tour of Europe. He had established a good reputation in our nation but felt that God was also calling him and his family to Europe. He wanted my help in seeing what might be possible for him. The request was made in a very good spirit, but I was hesitant at first - at least in my heart.

'Lord,' I prayed. 'I'm not even sure of my *own* family's future in Europe. How can I take someone else's call on board? Here we are looking for a place in Europe, not knowing where we'll live or how we'll survive, and my friend is asking me to help him with the same things.'

'I've worked hard and spent a lot of time to establish my relationships in Europe. Should I share the benefit of those relationships, the currency of that favour right now, when *we* are feeling so insecure? Besides, if I do this, and my friend also comes to Europe at the same time, won't that split the attention of people who might be able to help us in prayer and finances?'

You may think this sounds carnal, not very spiritual at all, but all these thoughts went through my mind. God had taken us through a great deal to prepare us to leave our large work in Australia and start again in Europe. I wanted to do it right.

Well, in spite of my initial reservations, I agreed to take my friend's cause on board. You see God began to take me on a journey of revelation; he put me through a course of life study. He began to school me in the subject of his own generous spirit. True excellence, he told me, is a generous spirit that pushes you beyond what is normal, or what is expected.[3] He told me that, if I was willing to represent my friend's interests - especially when my own situation was so precarious - I would be demonstrating a spirit of excellence. He would bless me for it.

I can tell you that God has blessed our family - and the Next W@ve International mission we started across Europe. We have had to run hard just to keep up with the favour he has given. Today, my friend is also blessed. He is running a successful and growing work that is changing the face of many churches in northern Europe and he is highly respected wherever he goes. As a friend, he also has my best interests at heart.

God answered my prayers in a way I had not expected. He answered a question with a question: was I willing to act in line with *his revelation* rather than *my need* alone? I took that revelation on board and I'm grateful that I did. God not only met those practical needs, he gave me something much more valuable - a window into his nature and the way he operates. I look back on that time as one of the most impacting in my Christian growth, as I received some powerful *information about God* and *impartation from him* that continues to influence my choices even today. That revelation was a greater gift than I'd expected to receive when I started praying for his prosperity in my life.

Make God's Priorities Your Priorities

When we waved goodbye to our homeland, we set up our home in Copenhagen, Denmark. It is a very charming old city with a long history and friendly, down-to-earth people. I'd visited the city a number of times before, speaking at conferences and the like.

One of the very first things I learned about the Danes is this: they're great cyclists! Take a drive in just about any part of Denmark and you'll find people getting about on two wheels. Young and old, they're at it. In all kinds of weather, they're at it. In the countryside and the city, they're at it. City roads in Denmark have special cycle lanes - alongside the separate car and bus lanes - and, if you hit a cyclist with your car, you can expect the full weight of the law to come down on you!

The second thing I discovered was this: Danes ride like Vikings on speed! Cycling sounds like such a genteel way to travel. The word conjures up pictures of smiling people gliding sedately along the road without a hint of aggression. That's *not* the way it is in some parts of Denmark! Danish cyclists have no fear. One of the most dangerous things you could do on a visit to Copenhagen is to stop in the middle of a cycle lane while the traffic is moving. Even worse would be to try to ride in the opposite direction! You've got to stay in the direction of the traffic.

A Hebrew word for this is *shalem*, which means 'in harmony with', or 'in the same direction as'. It's a word that is linked to *shalom*, which to most people means 'be at peace'. Shalem is used in 2 Chronicles 16:9:

> *'The eyes of the LORD range throughout the earth to strengthen those whose hearts are fully committed to him.'*

God is looking for people whose hearts are *shalem* with his heart, people who are in harmony with him. Or, if you like, people who are travelling in his direction, people who share his priorities. Another word for priorities is values. Your values are the priorities that influence your decisions and behaviour. Your upbringing, education and environment help to shape those values. For Christians, however, the most important values in our lives must be shaped by the Word of God. We must be working to line up our choices with God's choices, so that we are open to receive revelation.

If we are to be people of revelation, one of the most important values we need to work on is that of giving. You see, all revelation requires a degree of mystery. You can't be open to revelation if you think you already have all the answers! All revelation requires that we yield control to Someone who is greater than we are, who knows more than we do.

I used to wonder why the Lord placed the tree of the knowledge of good and evil in the Garden of Eden.[4] I mean, why put the thing there if it could cause all that trouble? If you look at the Genesis story, you'll notice that this was the only tree from which they could not eat. Every other tree was theirs - even the 'tree of life'![5]

I now believe that when God planted the tree he was asking human beings a question: 'Can you live with mystery?' He wanted to know if they were willing to let him be in control of the process of their development, or whether *they* had to have control, playing God. The Bible is clear: it's only when we give control to God that we exercise faith - and without faith it is impossible to live a life that is pleasing to God, that squares with God's view of your destiny.[6]

When we give something - our time, money, encouragement, anything - we are taking our hands off it and ceding control of it to someone else. When we give to God, we are practising a behaviour he loves very much: we are yielding control to him. *Then* we are open to revelation.

Have A Clean Imagination

Take another look at Deuteronomy 8:3:

> *'Man shall not live by bread alone, but by every word which proceeds from the mouth of God.'*

In the Hebrew original of this verse, there is no word for 'word'. What it says is something like this: '[Man lives] by every *proceeding forth* from the mouth of God.' So what, you say? So, revelation does not first come to us in words. Revelation comes not to the rational but to the *intuitive* part of our psyche; the part where images are formed.

The human imagination is very special to God. Today, we speak of 'self-image' and 'body-image'. We understand the importance of having healthy mental images or, if you like, 'imaginations'. The Bible tells us that the imagination is a precious gift from God and one that we must guard carefully. In fact, the human race's problems with sin began with wrong imaginations. Genesis records the serpent's conversation with Eve, and her reaction:

> *"'You will not surely die," the serpent said to the woman. "For God knows that when you eat of it your eyes will be opened, and you will be like God, knowing good and evil." When the woman saw that the fruit of the tree was good for food and pleasing to the eye, and also desirable for gaining wisdom, she took some and ate it. She also gave some to her husband, who was with her, and he ate it. (Genesis 3:4-6)*

Once the serpent spoke to her, Eve took another look at the tree. It was the same tree - it had not changed. Yet, she now had a different image of it. Her *imagination* had changed: she had lined up her mental image of the tree with the one Satan wanted her to have. That's why the Bible says God helps us to, 'demolish arguments and every pretension that sets itself up against the knowledge of God'. It commands us to 'take captive every thought to make it obedient to Christ'.[7] We must keep our imagination free of impure thoughts or ungodly images, so that we are 'online' to receive revelation.

Do As God Did: Become Human!

Notice one other thing here: if revelation first comes to the intuitive part of me, it is not God but me who puts words on that revelation. *I* am the one who chooses the words to express the picture or impression God is giving me.

Paul taught the Corinthian Christians that the real beauty of revelation gifts like prophecy is that they are uncluttered and easy to understand.[8] So, why do we so often clutter them up?

I grew up in a church environment where you were supposed to identify a word from God by the eloquence with which it was given. People used fancy-sounding words, or dramatic gestures, to show that God was truly speaking through them. Some preachers huffed, puffed and basically hyperventilated their way through a prophecy or other word from God, as if the Lord needed a little 'show-biz' to get the job done. As a result of this kind of thing, many Christians were discouraged from seeking after spiritual gifts. Many of us thought that things like prophecy, word of wisdom or word of knowledge were only for those 'experts' in the church who knew how to speak with heavenly oratory, or had a major breathing problem!

Yet, the Bible tells us something different:

'Follow the way of love and eagerly desire spiri-tual gifts, especially the gift of prophecy.' (1 Cor 14:1)

This instruction is for *every* believer, not just an elect few who happen to have loud voices in church. The Amplified Version of this verse says that we should 'cultivate' spiritual gifts: we should actively work on them, just like someone works on a garden.

How do you know a revelation word is really from God? Not by the clever words people wrap around it, or by the stagecraft of some preacher. You know it's God when it's accurate and when it changes a life, bringing encouragement, strength and comfort and leading people closer to Jesus.[9] Basically, it's the *genuine* article, when it makes God famous in someone's life!

Sometimes, God says to us: 'Why don't you just be natural, and let me be supernatural? I've been doing it a lot longer than you have. I wrote the book on supernatural. I *invented* supernatural!'

'Why don't you just do as I did - become *human*?'

God doesn't have to impress people with the way he talks. That takes the pressure off. We can be naturally supernatural when we share a revelation word.

Risky Business

I've had the privilege of sharing words of prophecy with people of all ages right around the globe. Prophecy, word of knowledge and word of wisdom are three manifestations of the Holy Spirit Paul talks about in 1 Corinthians. They are ways in which God makes himself known to people. If you hear someone give a prophecy, either to a group or an individual, and that prophecy is clearly accurate because it describes where the person is at, that is God saying, 'This is what I'm like.'

I never cease to thank God for the wonderful experience of watching people's lives change for the better almost before my eyes. Paul taught that prophecy lays bare the secrets of men's hearts.[10] Prophecy says to people: 'God is real. He sees you as an individual. He cares about the smallest details of your life and has answers for your greatest problems.'

Here's what Paul says:

'...Everyone who prophesies speaks to men for their strengthening, encouragement and comfort.' (1 Corinthians 14:3)

According to Paul, prophecy encourages people - literally, it gives people back their courage. The secrets God reveals are not usually those that will shame us, but those that will lift us to a new level of effectiveness and hope.

One time, I was preaching at a major conference event in Stockholm, Sweden. At the end of the message, I felt a strong impression that I should pray with man who was seated over to my left. We had a large crowd that night, and I invited the man to the front. As he came, I realised something that I've experienced many times before and since - I didn't have a clue what I was going to say to him! Obedience is an unconditional thing: you can't obey God only when you understand what he's up to. You must obey him even when you have no idea of the final outcome.

Once the man got to the front, the Lord gave me another strong impression, which I then put into words.

'You've been saying that your best days are behind you,' I told him. 'Your greatest desire has always been to resource the kingdom of God, yet in recent times, through a series of events, you have lost a great deal. Now, you say, your best days are gone.'

'But the Lord wants you to know that your best days are still ahead. He will restore to you what you have lost, and more. You will resource the sending of the gospel to the nations, just as you had dreamed of doing.'

The man, well dressed and groomed, broke down and began to weep as we prayed together. Later, my interpreter informed me that he was this man's pastor.

'You just read that guy's mail!' he told me. 'You described, with great accuracy, this man's experience over the past year.'

'You see, this man had been a successful businessman - one of Sweden's top entrepreneurs. He was making a lot of money and giving a lot of it to facilitate world outreach. But just this year, a series of business problems caused him to lose almost everything he had.'

'Mal, this very week, he sat in my office and poured out his heart to me. He said: "Pastor, my best days are behind me." You couldn't have known any of that, except God showed you. This is going to change his life!'

God definitely broke through in that man's situation. He gave courage and strength to a man drowning in despair, all through a simple revelation word. A few months later, I was in town again, and I had breakfast with that businessman. He shared how God had turned things around for him. He is once again making millions of Swedish Crowns each year, and using much of it to pay for Christian outreach. I was glad I'd stepped out in faith!

I could fill another book with stories like these. God loves to work in this way - to surprise people with his deep knowledge of their problems and his great hope for their future. Every time he speaks, he requires that I exercise faith by taking a chance.

God is omniscient. There is nothing that is unknown to him. When I step out of my 'known' into my 'unknown', I may have severely taxed *my* resources, but I've hardly started on his! Risk is the doorway into the exhilarating world of revelation.

Have A Passion For People

Real, godly revelation always comes in response to human need. It is *conceived* in mystery, but *birthed* in history. It always looks for a practical outlet.

If you've been in church life for more than a few weeks, you've probably heard talk about God's 'anointing' on people's lives. We talk about someone who is 'anointed to pray for the sick', or someone who's 'anointed to preach'. What exactly *is* 'anointing'?

In the Old Testament, anointing oil was poured on someone's head in special ceremonies, or at times of special significance. Anointing with this specially manufactured oil, which was never used for any other purpose, signified two things. Firstly, that a person was being set apart by God for a special calling or purpose. This was a sign for the people themselves, for those they would lead and for God. Secondly, it signified that they would possess certain special gifts from God to carry out that purpose.

Two groups of people were anointed in this way: kings (for practical leadership) and priests (for spiritual worship). [11]

The prophet Samuel poured anointing oil over Saul, setting him apart as the king of Israel. That day, the Spirit of God came upon Saul in a way he had not experienced before. Suddenly, he was able to prophesy like one of the holy men of Israel. [12] When David was anointed king, he too was visibly changed by the power of God. People could see that the Spirit of God was upon him in an unusual way. [13] Whenever God calls a person to a position of leadership, he also anoints them to fulfil that role. He gives them a platform from which to speak; a favour that causes people to open up to their influence.

To Moses, God gave an anointing for miracles, so that both the people of Israel and the king of Egypt would take heed to him. To Elijah and Elisha, God gave unusual prophetic insight and the ability to heal the sick. Again, the people were inspired to hear these men because of the evident favour of God upon them.

In the New Testament, Jesus is called the 'Anointed One'. [14] He was, above all men, anointed by God - set apart and empowered for a special purpose. Right from the beginning of his public ministry, Jesus was aware of his unique anointing, and of the purpose for which it was given:

> *'The Spirit of the Lord is on me, because he has anointed me to preach good news to the poor. He has sent me to proclaim freedom for the prisoners and recovery of sight for the blind, to release the oppressed, to proclaim the year of the Lord's favour.'*
> *(Luke 4:19)*

Jesus was set apart and empowered to do all of these things and he always gave credit for the works he did to

God the Father.[15] Yet the story of anointing doesn't stop with Jesus' death and resurrection. The New Testament goes on to say that the special empowerment that was present in Jesus' life now rests upon a whole community of people, the church. Today, we are God's kings and priests, called to leadership and to worship.[16] Today, none of us possesses all the anointing, the power, that rested on Jesus. We each individually reflect a different aspect of the ministry Jesus had when he was here.[17]

Some of us show that we are set apart and empowered to heal the sick, others that we are anointed to work miracles. Still others are specially gifted and called to preach. How do you identify your particular aspect of Jesus' anointing? Simple: by how God meets needs through you. You are anointed for a special purpose; to meet needs through the supernatural power of God.

'... You have an anointing [literally charisma, a special endowment of the Spirit] from the Holy One, and all of you know the truth.' (1 John 2:20)

Anointing is not a feeling; the kind of spine-tingles you get when you hear a certain kind of music, or stand in a certain type of atmosphere. What we sometimes *call* 'anointing' is really just ambience, or even emotion. Those things can be a *product* of anointing, but they're not the anointing itself.

Anointing is the manifest presence of God in response to human need. It is God saying, 'This is what I am like'. Whenever someone is healed in Jesus' name, that is God announcing himself as the great Healer. When someone is released from the oppression of a demonic power, God is saying, 'This is what I do, I deliver people and set them free.'

God's anointing on your life is how he supernaturally meets needs through you. It is more than your natural gifts and motivations. It is how God 'turns up' in supernatural ways when you pray for others. It is how God empowers you to do the supernatural works of Jesus, in response to concrete human needs.

The manifestations of God's Holy Spirit are not given to make *us* look good. Jesus steadfastly refused to work miracles just for show or to boost the size of his crowd. The supernatural, revelation gifts of God come to make *God* look good, which he is! They're given through us, to meet the needs of others and make God's name great. If we're going to release the anointing that God has put within us, we'll need to develop a passion for people and a commitment to bringing relief to hurting lives and broken hearts.

My friend Ray McCauley pastors the largest church in South Africa. He says that, 'The church is not relevant because it plays a certain type of music. The church is relevant because it meets human needs.' I once asked the great healing evangelist Reinhard Bonnke what motivates him to preach and pray for so many hundreds of thousands of people each year. His reply was simple: 'I just see what the devil does to people, and I get so angry!' That's the kind of passion God honours with the release of revelation anointing.

There's one other quality that brings revelation power - power that overcomes Babylon's influence and makes God famous. But it deserves a chapter on its own....

1.   John 14:16
2.   John 18:38
3.   Luke 6:32-38
4.   Genesis 2:9
5.   Genesis 2:16-17
6.   Hebrews 11:6
7.   2 Corinthians 10:5
8.   1 Corinthians 14:1-18
9.   1 Corinthians 14:3
10.   1 Corinthians 14:25

11. Exodus 29:21; Leviticus 8:12, 30; Exod 40:15; 2 Chronicles 23:11
12. See 1 Samuel 10:1,6, 9, 11
13. 1 Samuel 16:13
14. Acts 4:26,27
15. John 10:32
16. 1 Peter 2:9
17. 1 Corinthians 12:4-14

6

PROVE IT!

These are the closing days of an old millennium - just a few days before the word 'Eternity' appears over Sydney. I'm watching a TV music show that seems about as weary as the outgoing century...

Hang on, here's something different: a number one pop song performed by a fifty-nine year old man! (We're talking 'Spice Grannies' here.) A number one hit which the enlightened music gurus of radio and TV are deliberately ignoring because, they say, it's 'too cliched' for their discerning and sophisticated audience.

Admittedly, the tune is a little corny. And the lyrics, far from being new, were actually written almost 2000 years ago. They were composed by a man who'd never even heard a pop song. Yet his life and his words echo down through the centuries to touch our lives in a way no song ever could.

The song has, apparently, sold millions of copies in the U.K., across Europe, in Australia and in many other nations. It's been at the top of the British charts for weeks.

Set to the tune of *Auld Lang Sine*, and featuring lyrics from the Lord's Prayer, Cliff Richard's *Millennium Prayer* was an odds-on flop from the time it was released. Yet it sold millions of copies. Why? Because it struck a chord in people's hearts. People are still hopeful that there might just be a benevolent someone out there that, in the words of the Bette Midler song, watches us 'from a distance'. What they hope for, we Christians have! The apostle John, who learned prayer from the Master of prayer, wrote:

' *This is the confidence we have in approaching God: that if we ask anything according to his will, he hears us. And if we know that he hears us - whatever we ask - we know that we have what we asked of him.' (I John 5:14-15)*

It's part of our inheritance as God's children that, when we offer prayers in faith and obedience, we *will* receive an answer. A new level of revelation is always preceded by and accompanied by a new level of prayer. A daily discipline of prayer was a fundamental part of Daniel's lifestyle in Babylon. This is what made him available for special revelation.

In Hebrews, we read this about the great heroes of the Bible:

'... Through [their] faith [they] conquered kingdoms, administered justice, and gained what was promised ... ' (Hebrews 11:33)

When it says they 'gained' what was promised, the word used means to reach out and grasp. Literally, these men and women just reached out and *grabbed* the promises that God had made them. Imagine there was a spiritual Internet from which you could download health, peace of mind, joy, prosperity, wisdom and revelation. Would you be logging on? Sure you would. Is there any such thing? Yes, there is. God's Word is his Internet of the spirit. It is filled with all kinds of resources, or promises, that are available to us as Christians. All we need to do is 'download' them.

To connect to the physical Internet, you need a modem. It's the same with God's Internet of the spirit. Faith is the modem that connects me with God's promises and downloads their power into my life. The password is my obedience. It's an easy password to conveniently forget, but without it we can't make proper use of God's supernatural resources.

Getting A Result!

The apostle James told us that there are only two reasons why a Christian's prayer may not be answered.

Either it's because we don't ask - we tell the pastor, we complain to our wife or husband, we inform our friends, but we never get around to bringing it to the Lord! Or, it's because we ask with wrong motives.[1]

So, there *is* a right way to pray. There *is* a type of prayer that gets answers - and there's another that does *not*. The disciples of Jesus recognised this. Being part of a very religious culture, they'd seen many kinds of prayer before they met Jesus. They'd seen the self-righteous ramblings of the religious leaders, who loved to make an ostentatious show of their piety. Some of them had also watched John the Baptist at prayer. No doubt, he was all sincerity, passion, conviction and authority. As far as *styles* of prayer were concerned, the disciples already had a good education. Yet, they were so inspired by Jesus' kind of prayer that they insisted he teach them what he knew. What was it that attracted them to prayer the way Jesus did it?

Simply this: in all their years of watching different people at prayer, they'd never seen anyone *get results from prayer* like Jesus did!

God is a 'holy pragmatist'. He always looks for results. As we've already seen, there is a sense in which pragmatism can work against truth, by assuming that because something seems to work in the short term, it must be right. Yet there *is* a pragmatism which is very a godly thing. Our lives are meant to get a result for God. We're not meant to end our days holding in our hands nothing more of eternal worth than when we began.

In Luke 19, Jesus related the story of a nobleman who called his servants to himself and issued them each a sum of money. Before he departed on a long trip to a distant land, he gave them just one instruction: 'Put this money to work until I come back.'[2] The key word in this sentence is an interesting one. It is the Greek word from which we get 'pragmatic'. It means to busy yourself, or to trade. Basically, the nobleman in Jesus' story was telling his employees this: 'Make a profit until I return.'

When he did return, Jesus said, the nobleman

found that while two out of three of his servants had invested his money and seen it grow, the third had hidden his share in a field where, predictably, it did nothing! The first two were commended for their entrepreneurial attitude, and rewarded with even more property to oversee. The third suffered the ignominy of having the little he did possess taken away. Obviously, he was not to be trusted with even a very small investment.

Jesus said that this is a parable about how God's kingdom works. When Jesus returns, as Lord of the house, he will expect to find that we've made a profit on his initial investment. He'll want to see that we've taken what was entrusted to us and made it grow.

Everything Jesus did got a result. When he healed people, they stayed healed. When he cast out demons, they stayed cast out (unless the person went back to their old sinful ways).

When Jesus prayed, he got results too. Notice his prayer as they rolled away the stone from the tomb of Lazarus:

> 'Then Jesus looked up and said, "Father, I thank you that you have heard me. I knew that you always hear me, but I said this for the benefit of the people standing here, that they may believe that you sent me."' (John 11:41-42)

Now, *that's* a prayer filled with confidence: a confidence all the more evident when he turns and commands Lazarus to come out!

The disciples had never seen this kind of pragmatic, prayer-that-always-gets-results. They'd never seen prayer that without fail made a profit for the kingdom of God and made God famous. So, they asked Jesus to teach them *his* brand of prayer - prayer that proved what he could do. Jesus gave them a model prayer - a blueprint, or pattern, for pragmatic prayer that gets results.

Have you ever bought anything from one of those clever Scandinavian-style furniture stores? The furniture always looks good assembled in the showroom, but you can't carry it home that way. What you get is a box

MAL FLETCHER

full of parts and a bunch of diagrams to help you put it all together. It's do-it-yourself assembly.

That's what Jesus' model prayer is - an easy-to-remember, practical DIY (do it yourself) guide to putting together prayers that get results! All you need to do is follow the instructions.

Hallowed?

Right in the opening sentence of his model prayer, Jesus gives us the two primary foundations of all effective prayer:

'This, then, is how you should pray: "Our Father in heaven, hallowed be your name."' (Matthew 6:9)

1. Prayer begins and ends with God.

Many Christian leaders say, 'God is about to do something new in the world.' How can they possibly know that?

The first sign that God is planning something fresh in any generation is that his people begin to pray with a new urgency and passion. Before God moves in a city or a nation, he first moves his people to prayer.

John Wesley understood this. He said there have been great revivals without much preaching, but there's never been a great revival without much praying. He should know - some historians have credited him and his Methodist movement with saving England from bloody revolution. In six years during the 1780s, the Methodist movement grew from just 20,000 to over 90,000 people, in the U.S. alone. That's amazing growth in the days before mass media and jet travel - especially when you consider that the U.S. was not Methodism's home turf, which was in England.

Every day, Wesley would get out of bed to pray at 4 AM before he started preaching to workers in open fields at 5 AM. He would then get on his horse and travel up to four thousand miles every year, preaching and teaching as he went. Wesley was a gifted organiser and writer, but the foundation of his work was prayer.

Here's the bottom line: *prayer is God moving us to move him to move among us!* In Isaiah 43:19, the Lord gave Israel the good news that, despite all their past sin and woes, he was about to restore their fortunes:

> 'See, I am doing a new thing! Now it springs up; do you not perceive [literally, answer] it? I am making a way in the desert and streams in the wasteland.'

Then, just a little while later, he tells them how they should respond to this good news:

> 'You who call on the LORD, give yourselves no rest, and give him no rest till he establishes Jerusalem and makes her the praise of the earth.' (Isaiah 62:6-7)

My religious education taught me that prayer was mainly about *God* answering *me*. Yet the Bible says that prayer is as much about *me* answering *God*! He prophetically announces what he is about to do; he reveals some plan or purpose to me. Then he waits for *me* to answer *him.*

Have you ever played a team sport with people barracking wildly for you on the sidelines? When your side is heading down the field or court toward another goal, the cheers get louder and louder until they reach fever pitch. The crowd can see where you're headed and they're right there to get behind you.

God is looking for people who will see where he's headed - what goals he is going to score - and will cheer it on. He wants people who, when they gain an insight into where he's taking them, respond by saying, '*Yes* God! This is great! Come on, God - go for it! *I* want some of that action. Get *me* out there on the field, Lord. I'm ready to score for you!'

All over the world right now, Christians are organising for prayer as they have never done in our time. New prayer meetings are starting in houses of government, in universities and private homes - even in churches! There are twenty-four hour, seven-days-a-week prayer chains linking intercessors warriors via the Internet. (One of them advertises 'non-stop prayer across the nations for a generation lost in space.'[3]) In many high schools, students gather around the flagpole to pray for their cities and nations. There are men's prayer meetings, women's prayer days and prayer events in football stadiums. Who is behind this new drive for corporate prayer? Is it some ecumenical committee, or some international missions conglomerate? No, God himself is behind it. He's moving us to move him so that he can answer our prayers and move among us!

2. Prayer is about making God famous.

What does it mean to 'hallow' someone?

I remember when I first noticed my wife, Davina. Of course, she wasn't my wife then, but I remember a time when I first started taking a real interest in her, in what she was doing and thinking. There were other girls around at the time. Quite quickly, though, this one girl rose above the average, at least as far as I was concerned. To me, she was no longer commonplace, she was special. Davina was 'hallowed' in my eyes. I thought about her all the time.

The kind of prayer Jesus was teaching us lifts God's name above the commonplace; it makes people think again about God and his power. How does prayer honour God's name? By proving what he can do.

George Muller raised up some of the first and finest orphan houses in Britain. This German Christian personally took responsibility for feeding and housing scores of children every day, plus his staff. There were many occasions when a member of his dedicated crew would greet him with the cheery news that, 'There is no bread left today', or, 'We have nothing for the children to drink.'

What did George do? Did he publish a newsletter, construct a database and 'do a mail-out'? Did he buy air-time on national Christian TV? Answer: none of the above. For one thing, the technology wasn't there, but, more importantly, George had a better way of getting results. No matter what the urgent need, he would invariably slip on his hat and coat and go for a long walk. On his way out the door, he would announce to his workers that he was 'going to talk to Father about this.'

Time after time, George would return from his prayer walk to find that a load of bread had been delivered, or some new furniture had arrived, or some money had been received in the mail. George Muller's prayers honoured God because they proved what he could do.

Question: what are we praying for that really *needs* God's intervention? Many people spend their time praying for things they could just as easily get for themselves:

'Lord, I need a friend!'
'Well, go encourage someone.'
'Lord, I need some money.'
'Well, go look for a job.'

Think about it: why should God bother to answer a prayer you and I can't be bothered answering ourselves, when it is in our power to do so? Those prayers are not honouring to God. Prayer is not about showing what *I* can do, but proving what *God* can do. It's not wrong to ask God for *help* with things like friendship and money, not at all. It's just not very honouring to God if I'm asking him to get involved when I can't be bothered investing my own time.

What are we praying for that is beyond human capacity to perform? God is waiting for people who will give him an opportunity to show his muscle, who will believe for things that could not happen unless God did them! He is looking for individuals and churches that will believe promises that could only be fulfilled if God made them.

Your Kingdom.com

Some people use prayer like they use Amazon.com - they fill their shopping trolley with goodies that glitter and sparkle, then they take it all to the check-out and hope God will pass it through at his expense. It's true; we do have a credit account with God. Jesus swapped his life for ours and all the 'good credit' he had gained with God, through a life of total obedience and faith, was passed on to us through the cross.

However, prayer is not primarily about me getting what I want; it's about God getting what *he* wants. What *does* God want? He wants to establish his Kingdom.

The kingdom of God was always Jesus' first priority. He spoke of it over one hundred times in the gospel records, yet he mentioned the word that we translate as 'church' (the Greek word *ekklesia*) on only three occasions. Does that mean that the church is not important to the Lord? Not at all - in fact, the local church is the basic building block of God's kingdom, just as the family is the building block of a nation. Jesus himself made a regular habit of being in church and the writer to Hebrews is adamant that we should never get out of that habit![4]

What Jesus is showing us is that building the kingdom must be our first priority. We build churches to build the kingdom. We build businesses to extend the kingdom. We sow offerings and financial gifts to expand the kingdom. We raise our children, passing to them the values of the kingdom. *It's all about the kingdom.* So, what *is* the kingdom of God?

1. The kingdom of God is wherever God's will is done.

The kingdom is not a geographical location. There is no Kingdom of God Airport. God's kingdom is wherever people have made pleasing God their highest goal and greatest pleasure. It is where people pray, even in the toughest situations, 'not my will but yours be done.'[5] It's where men and women are prosperous in the true Bible sense of the word.

There's a lot of talk about prosperity in some sections of the church. If you read the Bible without religious blinkers on, you'll see that God does promise his people a prosperous life. There are many scriptures on that subject, enough to cover a book on their own. That God wants to prosper us is not open to question - but how you *define* prosperity is. Some people define prosperity as an outward show of success, measured by wealth and status. Other people take the opposite extreme: for them, a truly prosperous Christian is one who has abandoned all interest in material things and lives in self-inflicted poverty. Actually, there *is* a biblical measure for godly prosperity, but it's quite different from these. What *is* Bible prosperity?

A favourite verse with many preachers is 3 John 2, which says:

> *'Beloved, I pray that you may prosper in all things and be in health, just as your soul prospers.'* (New King James Version)

The word translated 'prosper' here, is made up of two little words in the Greek original. The first means 'good' and the second means 'journey', or 'progress'. John is praying that the people will 'make a good progress' even as their souls 'make good progress'. How does a soul make progress; what journey does a soul undertake? It's the journey of growth in the will of God: our soul makes progress in the plan of God for our lives.

Romans 8:28 is probably my father's favourite verse, and one I heard often as a child:

> *'And we know that in all things God works for the good of those who love him, who have been called according to his purpose.'*

It's interesting to note that the word 'his' doesn't appear in the original Greek. Literally, it says we are called 'according to purpose'. God called you *with purpose.* You were called to march to a different drum, to live by a higher sense of destiny than others do. The greatest good we can enjoy is to know that we are constantly going forward in the purposes God has for our lives. That's *real* prosperity. It's a theme repeated in Hebrews:

> *'May the God of peace ... equip you with everything good for doing his will, and may he work in us what is pleasing to him, through Jesus Christ, to whom be glory for ever and ever.' (Hebrews 13:20-21)*

A prosperous life is one that pleases God. That's what God's kingdom is all about.

2. The kingdom of God is where the rule of Christ is transforming lives.

You could say that the kingdom of God is a place of mercy, justice, peace, equality and dignity for all. That would be true. Every great social reformer in history has been working toward those ideals. Yet, many have tried to achieve these things through politics, economics, education and so on, without any reference to God at all.

There can be no kingdom without the king! Jesus told his disciples that the kingdom of God had arrived among them - that it was no longer some far off dream, but a present reality. Jesus could say that because he *was* the kingdom, in personal form. Everything the kingdom represents was summed up in him.

The kingdom of God is wherever the love and rule of Christ are transforming human hearts, relationships and institutions, and calling people of faith into community.

The way to extend God's kingdom on earth is first by spreading the influence of its king - by promoting Jesus at every opportunity.

A few years ago, we launched one of our citywide outreach events in Tallinn, the capital of Estonia. Church growth in this former communist stronghold is still a new phenomenon, and bold Christian evangelism is definitely something different.

For our first event in this city, we hired the largest nightclub in that part of Europe, a place that could easily hold over one thousand people. The Christians of the city were inspired when they managed to sell almost one thousand tickets for their first evangelistic event. Of course, there were many members of the public who came just because this was their club.

We took over the entire establishment for a no-holds-barred, in-your-face outreach event that combined the very best contemporary music, with hi-tech sound, lighting and multi-media - and, of course, high energy preaching! The atmosphere in that club was charged with excitement and, as the night went on, a growing sense of God's presence.

We brought a great Norwegian band with us and raised up a local band to do a worship set. Then I shared an in-your-face message about the *real* Jesus, the one so few Europeans have ever heard about. I invited people to put their drinks aside and come stand on the dance floor to offer a prayer of commitment to Jesus. Over thirty people made a first-time dedication to Jesus that night and were individually introduced to someone from a good local church.

The next day I was at the airport to catch my flight home. A young woman took my ticket at the check-in desk. She was smiling from ear to ear.

'Have we ever met?' I asked her. 'You look familiar.'

'I should do,' she replied. 'I was standing right in front of you last night.'

That young woman had become a Christian in that nightclub. She'd gone there for a dance or a drink, but instead of Johnnie Walker, she'd found Jesus. For her, the kingdom of God was not in a cathedral, or a warehouse converted to a church; it was in a club. That's where Jesus started to rule in her life, that's where he started to transform her heart, her relationships, her whole environment!

Christian, when you leave church on Sunday, you can hardly take the entire local congregation home with you. And you certainly can't rock up to work on Monday morning with your whole local church in tow. You can, however, carry the influence of the kingdom - it's values and power - everywhere you go. That's why Jesus put the kingdom first.

3. The kingdom of God is where people with changed hearts go on to change the world.

Jesus taught his disciples that, once they put their faith in him, the kingdom came to dwell in them. 'The kingdom of God,' he told them, 'is within you.'[6] It's impossible to get into this kingdom until *it* gets into *you!*

Once the kingdom is born in us, though, it starts to look for a way *out.* The kingdom can't possibly *stay* within us. The power of God's kingdom is too majestic, too awesome to be bottled up in our flawed human jars of clay. It is constantly looking for ways to show the 'all surpassing power of God' to the world around us.[7] The power of God's kingdom seeks an outlet, so that it can change our world for the good.

That's what Paul meant when he wrote:

'Therefore my friends ... continue to work out your salvation with fear and trembling, for it is God who works in you to will and to act according to his good purpose.' (Philippians 2:12-13)

We 'work out' our salvation not by trying to analyse it or rationalise it - let's face it, we'll never fully understand why God saved us as he did. We 'work out' our salvation by allowing it to pervade every area of our lives, spreading its positive influence from our inner being into our daily environment and relationships.

Many professing Christians exhibit a knee-jerk reaction to these changing times, because they've adopted an escapist model for life. They don't want to face the real world in all its raw passion and pain; they'd rather live in a photo-retouched version of reality, where all the nasty bits have been airbrushed away.

They're escapist in their thinking on world outreach. 'Why should I get too involved in evangelism and personal soul-winning?' they say. 'After all, there's a revival coming when people will just be "swept" into God's kingdom.' (Remember: God will never do for us what he has called and equipped *us* to do for *him!*)

They're escapist in their approach to faith. 'Don't talk to me about long seasons of sowing,' they murmur. 'I just want to hear about the reaping part.'

And they're certainly escapist in their teaching on the last days of the human race. 'Why bother getting involved in changing the world? After all, Jesus is coming back soon - and, before that, there'll be the Antichrist.'

Some of these people are better escape artists than Harry Houdini! They run from reality and then claim that this is living 'by faith'. In fact, the Bible teaches the opposite. Real faith is *not* escapist in its thinking. It doesn't run from earthly problems, hiding its head under the bed of promise-box Christianity. Real faith is more robust, more athletic than that. It recognises the facts, but then looks beyond them to an even bigger 'Fact', who is God himself!

When David faced a nine foot six inch tall NBA basketball giant called Goliath, he didn't try to rationalise the challenge away ('I will not confess that Goliath is real, I will not confess that Goliath is real…'). He dealt with Goliath as a real fact. But he also saw, standing somewhere above and behind Goliath, a smiling God who was winking and saying, 'Come on son, let's take this sucker down!'

Abraham, the 'father of the faithful', is perhaps our best example of this principle:

> 'Without weakening in his faith, [Abram] faced the fact that his body was as good as dead - since he was about a hundred years old - and that Sarah's womb was also dead. Yet he did not waver through unbelief regarding the promise of God, but was strengthened in his faith and gave glory to God, being fully persuaded that God had power to do what he had promised. This is why "it was credited to him as righteousness."' (Romans 4:19-22.)

Abram - or, Abraham - faced the facts, but saw past them to fulfilment of God's promises.

In our time, we also have much to learn from committed Christian reformers like Mother Teresa and Martin Luther King. They passionately believed in and worked for God's kingdom. They proved that more can be accomplished by one person whose heart has been radically changed - through surrender to Christ - than by all the politicians and social activists put together!

Our prayers will get results - and make God famous - when we start putting the interests of the kingdom above our own, recognising that the kingdom of God is not just about heaven when we die, but extending the rule of Christ on earth in the here and now!

4. The kingdom of God is where God's Word rules.

If you use e-mail a lot, as most of us do these days, you're no doubt familiar with the term 'zip program'. If I decide to send you a large file - say, a photo or a graphic - as an e-mail attachment, I don't send it in its raw form, as it would take forever to upload and download. Depending on where you live, the phone bills might climb dramatically and we'd waste time waiting.

Instead, I use a piece of software to 'zip' the file, to compress it into a smaller and more manageable size. Then, when you've received it, you need to 'unzip' the file using another piece of software.

In some ways, the Bible is *God's unzip program*. When you became a Christian, you received all the power of God's kingdom within you, through the presence of his Holy Spirit. You became a part of the kingdom, and it became a part of you. Within you is the same power that caused Jesus to do amazing, miraculous things. However, you couldn't handle it if its full power were released within you all at once. You'd be fried to a potato chip on the floor; added to the wall paper pattern in your room. The 'file' is just too big for you to handle.

So, in a sense, God places the power of the kingdom within you in 'zipped' form. Then he gives you his unzip program so that you can apply the power of the kingdom as you need it. If you are sick, you can begin to read what the Bible says on divine health and healing. As you line up your actions with this, you begin to 'unzip' the power of the kingdom to bring healing to your body. If you are poor, you can study what the Scriptures say about divine blessing and, as you live out what it teaches, you 'unzip' the kingdom's power to receive blessing. And so it goes.

There are many Christian people who are not really experiencing the power of God's kingdom. Often, the problem lies with the fact that they're not reading *and* applying the truth of God's Word. Consequently, they're unable to apply its principles to their environment. God has nothing with which to *unzip* the power of the kingdom in their lives. We make God famous, and our prayers get a result, when we place more emphasis on *obedience* than *convenience.*

1. James 4:2-3
2. Luke 19:12-13
3. See www.24-7prayer.com
4. Luke 4:16 and Hebrews 10:25
5. Luke 22:42
6. Luke 17:21
7. 2 Corinthians 4:7

7

Living As If You Already Died

It's 1956. In America, young people are throwing off
the cares of their parents' war-ravaged generation.
They're hungry to have fun, to enjoy life. They've
started dancing to a whole new kind of music. At first,
it's all Happy Days innocence and fun. In time, though,
the hedonistic spirit of the age will lead them to
experiment with mind-altering drugs, and to try to
convince themselves that there really is such a thing
as 'free love'.

In the midst of this emerging Babylon, five young,
evangelical Christians hear a call from God. It's a
demanding call, a dangerous call, and a life-
consuming call. That's how they knows it's from God.

Jim Elliott is one of the five. He knows what he
must do. God is calling him to take the message about
Jesus to some of the remotest tribes-people of South
America, the Auca Indians (or Huaorani) of Ecuador.
These people have hardly ever seen a white man,
much less heard about Christ.

In simple obedience, Jim and his fellow
frontiersmen make the journey to their obscure mission field. They know the danger that may await
them, yet they boldly go where no Christian has gone
before.

On one of their first forays into the jungle, warriors
with spears ambush them. Five young Christians meet
their deaths that day.

Their bodies are flown back to the U.S., where the
press picks up the story. People are shocked that such
a thing should happen in modern times, to young
Americans who are seeking only to bring a message
of hope to a forgotten corner of the globe.

Some months after Jim Elliott's funeral, a friend cautiously approached his young widow. There was a question burning in his heart, yet he hardly dared give it voice.

'There's something I don't understand,' he stammered. 'I just can't explain it. How do you deal with the fact that Jim was killed that day in the jungle? How do you deal with the way he died? How can you handle that?'

The young woman looked him in the eye and, with little hesitation, replied: 'My Jim didn't die in the jungle that day.'

The grief is too much for her, he thought. She's not able to face reality - and who can blame her?

'No, Jim didn't die in the jungle,' she continued. 'My Jim died one night in high school, where he knelt by his bed in prayer. He said, "Jesus, if you did all this for me, there is nothing I can do for you that will ever repay the debt I owe. I commit myself here and now to go wherever you want me to go and do whatever you call me to do. I'm yours, do with me as you please."'

She paused. 'That's where my Jim died.'

What will change cities and reshape the spiritual landscape of nations and generations? It won't be our Christian music, no matter how good it is. It won't be our sophisticated conferences or hi-tech outreach programs. It won't be our satellite TV outlets, either. All of that is good, but what will *really* change our world is *Christians who live as if they are already dead!*

The world is looking for followers of Jesus who will live as he did - with a spirit of joyous self-sacrifice and self-denial. Not people who are *dead boring*, but *dead to self* and sin. Alive-to-God kind of people.[1] We serve people of all ages, Boomers, Gen-Xers and the Generation Next, who have grown up with the greatest special effects in movie history; people who play on their digital game consoles, knowing the difference between fantasy and reality, the fake and the real. In such an age, people are very sensitive to what is phoney. Who will make

God famous in an age like this? Those who live as if they are not their own, but bought with a price.[2]

Marching To A Different Drum

We've been looking into the subject of prayer. Without a habit of prayer there can be no prophetic lifestyle, no everyday experience of revelation, no making God famous. In age where people are crippled spiritually by their reliance on rationalism and humanism, revelation cuts through all the pretensions and makes God famous.

As we've seen, there is a kind of prayer that gets results, that honours or 'hallows' God's name. It proves what God can do and opens the heavens to the practical power of revelation. This kind of prayer was the focus of Jesus' teaching when he gave us the Lord's Prayer. Here's the line where we often opt out:

'Your kingdom come, your will be done on earth as it is in heaven.' (Matthew 6:10)

How is God's will done in heaven? Do they have a Divine Debating Society, where the angels weigh up the pros and cons of carrying out God's commands?

'Today, the subject for discussion is this: Should we or should we not obey the will of the Almighty? For the "yes" side, we have the cherubim, and for the "no's" we have the seraphim. You may begin...'

Is that how it works? Or, do the head angels conduct opinion polls to find out whether the majority favour doing as God says?

In heaven, the will of God is done without question, in faith. The angels don't always understand what God is doing or planning. They can't really comprehend, for example, God's love for *us* - any more than we can.[3] Yet they obey him, without question.

Let's be honest - we're in much the same predicament as the angels most of the time, only more so! We just don't understand. In Isaiah 55:9, God says:

*'As the heavens are higher than the earth, so are
my ways higher than your ways and my thoughts than
your thoughts.'*

In its literal Hebrew form, it reads something like
this: 'As the heavens *soar above* the earth, so my methods
and my plans *soar above* yours.'

That's our problem. Often when God speaks to us,
we either don't understand his plan, or we don't agree
with his way of bringing it to pass. Abraham didn't
understand when God told him to offer his only son as a
sacrifice. Yet, he obeyed.[4] Joshua didn't really get it when
God ordered him to walk around Jericho for seven days.
Yet, he obeyed.[5] Isaiah couldn't really grasp what God
was showing him about a suffering Messiah. After all,
his religious education told him that a Messiah was
destined to rule on the throne of David.[6] Yet he obeyed,
and penned one of the most moving passages of text
known to man - Isaiah 53.

Daniel didn't comprehend most of what he was
seeing in his vision of the end times.[7] Joel had no way
of grasping what God meant when he promised an
outpouring of his Spirit on all flesh.[8] After all, Israel were
God's chosen people, not the Gentiles. The apostle John
could have had no real understanding of all he was
seeing in his visions on Patmos.[9] Yet, in every case these
men obeyed - without question. They trusted more in
the integrity and wisdom of God than in their own sense
of what would be right or appropriate. That's why God
called them heroes of faith.

What *is* faith? It is lining up our decisions and
choices with God's decisions and choices, *especially*
when we don't understand his ways, or when we can't
control the outcome. Many Christians will obey as long
as they feel they have some control over how things turn
out. Real faith calls us to yield our right of control.

When we were created, we were meant to have the
joy of responsibility without the burden of ultimate
control. Our relationship with God was to be our security,
while he allowed us to have dominion over his creation,

to rule as kings and queens and shape its future.[10] Sin, however, ruined all that. At its root, all sin is about *control* - it's about human beings trying to control things that only God can or should control. That's why worry is a sin, because it's a form of surrogate control. When we worry, we are trying to change things that are, in fact, beyond us. We play with permutations and combinations in our minds, refusing to give control to God. It doesn't really change *anything*.

Likewise, bitterness is a sin, not just because it destroys relationships, but because it too is about control. I can't change what someone has done to me, or their attitude toward me, so I toy with thoughts of revenge. I play with the Rubik's Cube inside my head, imagining all sorts of permutations and combinations in which I get even and settle the score. It doesn't actually achieve *anything* - except to pull me further away from the nature of God. It simply offers a counterfeit, surrogate form of control. It leads me to try to control a situation that only God can resolve.

Prayer gets results and makes God famous when we obey God's voice without question, without needing to be in control.

The Missing Link

'Give us today our daily bread.' (Matt 6:11)

I don't know if you've ever noticed this: there's one thing missing in the Lord's prayer. You'd think that if anyone knew a thing or two about prayer, it would be the Son of God. Yet, he left out one major element. It's a significant one because it represents what most Christians spend at least half their prayer time doing.

There are no question marks in the Lord's prayer. Jesus doesn't waste his time with things like, *'Is it you will* to give me this day my daily bread?' Or, *'Is it your will* to forgive us our sins?' Many of us spend most of our prayer time asking questions like, 'Is this your will?', and 'Is that your will?'

Jesus' model prayer is a series of decisive statements based on what Word of God has already promised us. The Father has already covenanted to bless us with food.[11] He has already pledged to protect us from our enemies.[12] He's on record as saying that he will freely pardon us when we turn to him.[13] In praying for these things, Jesus is simply standing on promises God has already made to his people.

God would rather we pray in faith based on what we *do* know, than waste our time speaking out of doubt, basing our prayers on what we *don't* know. No, it's not wrong to ask God questions - he is, after all, the one with all the answers. But it's not productive to spend fifty percent of our prayer time doing it!

I said earlier, that God has provided us an 'Internet of the spirit', an opportunity for us to 'download' into our experience all his promises and resources. My faith provides the 'modem' to connect with those promises. Now, when my physical modem is turned on, there's an indicator on the PC to tell me it's doing its thing. How do I know my faith is at work, reaching out for God's promises?

One indicator is *boldness.* The Lord's prayer was offered with total confidence. There was nothing shy or timid about Jesus. Whether it was speaking to a storm, raising a dead man, throwing extortionists out of the Temple, or teaching against religious hypocrisy, everything he did was done *boldly.*

In Acts, the apostles were also known for their boldness. Acts 4:13 says:

> 'When [the Jewish leaders] saw the courage of Peter and John and realised that they were unschooled, ordinary men, they were astonished and they took note that these men had been with Jesus.'

What was it that made these guys look like followers of Jesus? It was their boldness. Theirs was a courage that didn't come from their training, or from any natural charisma on their part, it came from their living connection to Jesus. They knew that as long as they were doing the works of Jesus, they could be as bold as he had been. They were standing on solid ground. Mother Teresa was once asked how she felt about needing to raise money for her work. She said, 'As long as I'm doing Jesus' work, he will bring the money in. If the money stops, I must not be doing his work.' She was less than five feet tall, but she was bold - and she reached out to receive God's promises.

The other indicator that our faith is active is *persistence*. The Lord's prayer was meant to be offered many times over - we're taught to ask for *daily* bread, not monthly bulk deliveries!

When a woman becomes pregnant, she knows she has no ability to set the time limit for the baby's arrival. If the birth is a natural one, the baby will come when it is good and ready! The mother can't walk into the hospital ward and announce, 'OK baby, you've got ten minutes, then I go home to watch TV.'

Praying for a thing in faith is a little like being pregnant. When you start, you give up all rights to set the time limits. You have to keep praying until the answer arrives, or until God changes the prayer as he shows you more of his will. You can't abort the prayer until the answer is born.

Doing What You Can

'Forgive us our debts, as we also have forgiven our debtors.' (Matt 6:12)

Jesus often taught that if you don't forgive others, you shouldn't expect God to forgive you. In fact, he followed his model prayer with these words:

'For if you forgive men when they sin against you, your heavenly Father will also forgive you. But if you do not forgive men their sins, your Father will not forgive your sins.' (Matt 6:14-15)

The same principle holds true whatever you happen to be praying for. You need to ask yourself the question: Is my life in line with my prayer? How can I do my part? Is there something I need to change to help bring about the answer?

Standing on God's promises and reaching out to obtain them means more than having them locked in your mind. It means taking positive action, making room in your life so that you can accommodate the promises.

When a married couple hear that they're going to become parents, they don't sit back on the sofa and say, 'That'll be nice when it happens, until then we'll just sit back and drink tea.' There are changes to be made around the house. For one thing, there's a nursery to be prepared. You can't bring a child home and put it to bed in a cardboard box on top of the TV. You have to get things ready in advance, so that you can accommodate the new arrival.

When we start praying for something, we must get our lives ready to accommodate the answer. If I'm praying about a financial need, I should check my spending habits to see whether my budget is in order. If I'm spending more than I earn, or blindly charging everything to credit, I shouldn't expect prayer alone to solve my problems. If I'm praying about a problem in my marriage, I should evaluate whether I need to spend more time with my partner. If I'm praying through a problem with my children, I might need to spend more time with them, or listen more attentively to them.

Preparing for the answer may mean taking some things *out* of my life - removing blockages like a bitter spirit, or a cynical and negative attitude. Those things cause interference on the 'phone line' and make it difficult for my 'modem' to 'download' the promises of God.

Preparing for the answer might also mean putting some new things *into* my life - developing new habits of behaviour, or fresh ways of thinking and speaking.

Earlier, I spoke about my feelings when God called us to leave Australia and our ministry there to start again in Western Europe. We had prophecies, we had promises from the Bible, and we had clear signposts in our circumstances - everything indicated that God was about to do something new in our experience. One of the many words God gave us was a very simple one:

'Put out into deep water, and let down the nets for a catch.' (Luke 5:4)

Davina and I had some wonderful promises from the Lord, but we couldn't help wondering how on earth God could possibly fulfil them. After all, Europe is, for an Aussie, the 'uttermost part of the earth', and a move of this scale would in a way mean starting all over again. Despite our nervousness, we started to 'build the nursery'. I had been invited to speak at a series of large conferences, churches and events throughout Europe. All of them fell within a four-month period. We had also been planning a mission to Belfast, Northern Ireland - a place that had long been on my heart because of its Troubles.

Normally, I would have declined some of the invitations, but we decided that we wanted to give God some 'room to move' in taking us forward into our destiny. So, we moved to Europe for four months, taking our children from nation to nation, moving through a hectic itinerary of ministry. All the while we were asking, 'God, give us definite signs along the way, signs that you're setting things up for us in Europe.'

It was during that costly and often draining trip, that the Lord opened some miraculous doors which later allowed us to move our family for the long-term. If we hadn't taken that first big step, we would not have been 'on-line' when the promise came. We had acted to accommodate God's promises.

Remember: God's opportunity comes at your extremity. It's when you've done all you can do, that God steps in to take care of the rest. Our prayers will really honour and prove God when we act in line with our own requests.

How Not To Lose The Moon

Jesus continued his prayer:

'And lead us not into temptation, but deliver us from the evil one.' (Matt 6:13)

One of my favourite movies has to be *Apollo 13*. It's the true story of one man's dream - to walk on the moon. It had been his dream since childhood. He would gaze up at the skies at night and call up mental images of planting his feet in the moon dust.

As time went by, he was offered the chance to turn his dream into a reality. He became a test pilot and then qualified as an astronaut. Later, he was offered the command of a spacecraft that was destined for the moon.

His dream turned into a nightmare, though. The ship under his command went out of control mid-flight. NASA spent days wondering if it could ever bring its three astronauts back to earth.

In the movie, the commander, played by Tom Hanks, looks out the window at the moon and realises he will never see his dream fulfilled. 'Gentlemen,' he whispers to his crew, 'we have just lost the moon'.

What was the cause of problem on board? Had a huge comet smashed into the ship? Had a massive explosion torn it apart? No, the problem started with nothing more than a tiny valve that began to leak. One small problem led to another larger one, which led to yet another problem and so on.

One man's dream was left unfulfilled, a multi-million-dollar space mission was aborted, and billions of people around the world worried for days over the lives of three astronauts. All because of one leaky valve.

The Bible word 'sin' actually refers to an abuse of our God-given right to choose. If I choose things that are in harmony with God's character and nature, my life will be rich and blessed.[14] If I decide, however, to abandon those righteous choices, my life, while it may be pleasurable for a season, will ultimately end in isolation from God. [15]

Three things are always true about sin. It always takes you further than you wanted to go - you can't control how far it will carry you. It always keeps you longer than you wanted to stay - you can't control how long it will influence you. And it always costs you more than you're willing to pay - you can't control how much it will take from you.

The thing about sin is not what it *adds* to your life, but what it *takes away*. It removes a part of your God-likeness; it distorts the image of God in you. If you are a Christian, it pollutes the righteous nature Christ has given you.

As the time for Jesus' death drew near, he told his disciples:

> *'I will not speak with you much longer, for the prince of this world is coming. He has no hold on me, but the world must learn that I love the Father and that I do exactly what my Father has commanded me.'*
> *(John 14:30-31)*

'He has no hold on me.' The King James Version has it this way: 'he has nothing in me.' Jesus could even face death on a cross with confidence - because he knew that he and the devil had *nothing in common*. Satan had no *claim* on his life, no right to accuse him of sin and no place to find moral weakness.

Our prayers will get results and make God famous when we steer clear of the devil, the evil one, and deal with the 'leaky valves' in our lives - those small compromises that can bring our dreams to nothing.

1. Romans 6:11
2. 1 Corinthians 6:20
3. 1 Pet 1:12
4. Hebrews 11:17-19
5. Joshua 6
6. Isaiah 53
7. Daniel 10-12
8. Joel 2:28-29
9. The book of Revelation
10. Genesis 1:28
11. Deuteronomy 28: 4-5
12. Deuteronomy 23:14
13. Isaiah 55:7
14. Deuteronomy 28:1-13
15. See Proverbs 14:12 and Hebrews 11:25

Two roads diverged in a wood, and I -
I took the one less travelled by,
And that has made all the difference.

Robert Frost,
***The Road Not Taken*, 1916**

What once was hurt,
What once was friction;
What left a mark
No longer stings,
Because Grace makes beauty
Out of ugly things.

Bono, Grace, from U2's
***All That You Can't Leave Behind*, 2000**

For centuries, Christian values and teaching have had a profound influence in the world of art. Along the way, however, we've lost ground.

For Christians to have influence, to make God famous in a secular world like ours, we will need to do more than have strong devotional lives in private. Whilst the kingdom *is* born within us, by the Holy Spirit, God does not intend us to *keep* its power bottled up within our hearts or personal lives.

In each of this series of books, I will discuss one area where I believe Christians need to return to influence in a post-modern world. I will look at why we need to recapture ground we might have lost, and how this might be done. In particular, I want to investigate how individual Christians *can* make a difference.

In this book, the subject is Christianity and the arts. Perhaps you are an artist of some kind - with words, pictures, graphics, film, computer animation, or whatever. This section is definitely for you! On the other hand, you might be thinking, 'That's not me. I'm no artist.' Though you may not call yourself an artist, you *are* creative. God has gifted you with an ability to express his innovative nature in one way or another, whether through a business, a profession, a Christian ministry, or in building a family. Releasing this God-given creativity makes him famous. This section is for *all* God's creative people.

Mal Fletcher

8

Where Have All The Artists Gone?

*Here we are, at last. We've waited in a queue outside
the building for quite a while, trying to stay warm on
an unsettled spring day in Amsterdam.*

*My son, Grant and I are finally inside the famous
Van Gogh museum. We're gazing, with a horde of
other visitors, at a wall filled with Vincent's paintings.
It's awe-inspiring. What really strikes us is the
incredibly vivid use of colour. This man seems to have
had some extra wiring in his brain. It allowed him to
see hues and shades that are normally invisible to
lesser mortals like us!*

*As I stand there, I know I've seen all the poster
reproductions, but the real articles are snatching my
breath away.*

*As we leave the building, I glance over at the gro-
wing queue waiting to get in. I can't help wondering
why people don't line up for church like that.*

For the past twenty years, the world of art has been
going through a kind of renaissance and art's popularity
shows no sign of waning. Hotels, restaurants and
cinemas exhibit and sell works of art and Internet art
auctions do brisk business.

Sadly, many church leaders have come to view the
arts as something that exist 'out there', beyond the
purview or interest of the church. In many sections of
the church, we've relinquished our influence in an area
that shapes people's thinking and values. Our culture
suffers because we've taken preaching out of the
marketplace and art out of the church.

If we're ever to make God famous again in western
cultures, we *must* recapture some ground when it comes
to influence in the arts.

Art: Why Do We Like It?

What does art do for us? Why do we buy it, look at it and like having it around? I suppose there are some people who, because they are in a position to do so, think of art primarily as a financial investment. But what is it that gives art that resale value?

In everyday terms, we use the word 'art' to refer to human works in areas of aesthetic interest or beauty, particularly in literature, music, drama, painting, sculpture and architecture.

Historically, there are two major schools of thought that shape the way we think about art. Aristotle taught that is about *mimesis*, or imitation. It gives pleasure according to how accurately it represents the real world as we see it. Traditional portraits and landscapes are a good example of this approach to art.

Plato, on the other hand, said that artists are inspired by the *Muses* - by God or by inner feelings and impulses - to express things that are beyond the natural senses. Art reflects eternal truths, inner emotions and something of the essence of the age - what the Germans call the *zeitgeist*. Abstract and other forms of modern art are good examples of the role art plays in suggesting something deeper than what we actually see in nature. Of course, even traditional portraiture has the capacity to stir our emotions, to whisk us off to some 'other place'. In that sense, you could say that all art is 'inspired'.

Art can have a profound effect on our emotions. At different times, it amuses or provokes us; it soothes or unsettles us. Bernard Berenson, writing in 1897, made this statement about art: 'not what man knows but what man feels, concerns art. All else is science.'

Art operates on us at the level of what the Bible refers to as the soul. In the Greek language of the New Testament, the word often translated 'soul' is *psyche*. It refers to the 'immaterial, invisible part of man; ... the seat of the sentient element in man, that by which he perceives, reflects, feels, desires; ... the seat of will and purpose.'[1] Robert Beverly Hale said that art is, 'Breaking a hole in the subconscious and fishing there.'

In some cases, the New Testament word for 'spirit' - *pneuma*, or breath - means exactly the same thing. We might say that art has an almost spiritual effect in us. It may be the closest we can come to a truly supernatural experience using only the emotional and psychological parts of our make-up.

This is why art has been written, argued and commented about for centuries, and why it gives us so much sheer pleasure. This is also the reason why we should treat it with respect and approach it with discernment.

Art Has Power

The rise in art's importance is partly due to increased affluence and disposable income, at least in developed countries. More people than ever before can actually afford to enjoy - and create - works of art. It is also linked to the cry for transcendence that's emerging in this post-materialistic age. The age of rationalism in Europe robbed many people of opportunities to nurture the creative and intuitive side of the human psyche. Now, people are looking for ways to stimulate and feed the spiritual side of their nature.

These are uncertain times. In troubled times, seasons of rapid change, people tend to gravitate toward one of two extremes for their security. Either they head for religious fundamentalism, of the kind we see in some Islamic nations, or they find comfort in personal, spiritual experience.[2] The symbolism of a new millennium has left many people searching for some higher sense of purpose for the human experience. Art offers a different way of seeing and appreciating our selves and our environment, and even provides ideas on the meaning of our existence.

There are people, of course, will opt for a third path - hedonism. In times of great change, some people choose to believe that there *is* no underlying meaning in human existence. And if there's no point in it all, says the hedonist, we might as well cram as many pleasant experiences as we can into our short lives before the curtain falls, or the bomb drops. So, as one writer put it, we have invented the sixth human need - the need for novelty, for constant stimulation of the senses in new and exciting ways. Art can, for some people, provide some of that novelty.

If you're a Christian, you will see the upswing in spiritual interest in our society as a sign of real hope. You have good reason to see it as evidence of the fulfilment of divine promises; promises made through ancient seers like Joel:

> 'And afterward, I will pour out my Spirit on all people. Your sons and daughters will prophesy, your old men will dream dreams, your young men will see visions. Even on my servants, both men and women, I will pour out my Spirit in those days.' *(Joel 2:28-29)*

A purely materialistic, rationalistic generation can never know the God of the Bible, for he is experienced through faith. Faith involves a certain use of sanctified imagination. It's about perceiving what is not yet seen.[3]

Art Owes The Church

Whatever you think of the church, you cannot ignore the contribution Christian stories, teachings and ideas have made to the development of the arts in the western world. From painting and sculpture to architecture and music, Christianity has been a major influence in the development of western art.

You can't overestimate, for example, the contribution of Christianity to the world of music. When J. S. Bach wrote many of his most famous works, he scribbled on the manuscript the words *Soli Deo Gloria* ('to God alone be the Glory'). His sacred music includes two hundred church cantatas, oratorios for Easter and Christmas, the two great *Passions* of *St. Matthew* and *St. John*, and the *Mass in B minor*. For the last seventeen years of his life he was the musical director at a religious choir school in Leipzig.

Many of George Frideric Handel's musical master-pieces also centred around Bible themes - as with *Israel in Egypt* (1739) - and characters - as in *Belshazzar* (1745), *Samson* (1743) and *Saul* (1739). His most celebrated work was, of course, the *Messiah* (1742).

Many other composers, including the awesome Beethoven and Haydn, invested time and energy in writing pieces for the church. Some, like Franz Liszt, even gave part of their lives to full-time religious service.

Of course, some people might argue that composers only produced religious music because the church was one of the few social institutions that had the resources to support them. Certainly, that may have been the motivation of some. However, there many who, through the sheer bulk and quality of their religious works, revealed a strong empathy for the spiritual themes they were developing.

Christianity has had an enormous influence on painting, drawing and sculpture too. If you doubt it, one walk through any major European gallery will change your thinking. Such luminaries as Michelangelo, Da Vinci and Van Gogh all sculpted or painted using religious themes, or for religious settings. Buonarroti Michel-angelo, whose enormous talent dominated the High Renaissance period, made his name with amazing sculptures like his *Pieta* and *David*. The latter took him a full three years to complete. He also devoted four years to the frescoes in the Sistine Chapel.

In The Beginning

We can trace the influence of Christianity on western art right back to the very early days of the Christian faith.

When Christianity was made an official state religion, under Constantine, Roman artistic traditions began to be adapted to portray Christian symbols and saints. What followed in the east of the empire became known as the Byzantine period, named after the city of Byzantium, the focal point of the empire at that time. It later became known as Constantinople. Churches were decorated with mosaics and religious images were painted in glittering colour. Icon painting was also a feature of the time, and continues even today in places like Russia and Greece.

At the same time, Christian monasteries were turning out some of the most beautifully illustrated manuscripts ever seen. We can still see examples of this ornate art form in museums today - for example, the famous *Lindisfarne Gospels* in the British Museum. In places like Ireland, monk evangelists often incorporated symbols and designs from local tribal art into biblical texts, so the people could better identify with the message. The process of manuscript illumination continued right up to the invention of the printing press in 1450.

A century later, Romanesque art combined images drawn from nature with those from myth and religion. Beasts, medieval warriors and biblical heroes all battled for attention. In Gothic times, from the late twelfth to fifteenth centuries, stained glass production opened up a whole new art form. Huge panels of coloured glass lit up the vast cathedrals of the time, each one telling a Bible story or illustrating a spiritual truth. Even today, they're awe-inspiring.

The Christian faith also contributed much to the art of the scribe. In the days before the printing press, these gifted and hard-working craftsmen worked with nothing more than penknives, quills and parchment. Yet they created books that are, even in the age of digital photography, still considered things of rare beauty. Scribes saw their labour as a way of bringing greater glory to God.[4]

God Is In The House

Of all the arts, it's perhaps in architecture that we see the greatest witness for Jesus through the ages. Many a masterpiece of western building is dedicated to Christ.

Michelangelo served, for a time, as chief architect of the incredible St. Peter's basilica in Rome, adding its impressive dome. He also left us the Sistine Chapel's beautiful ceiling motif and the vast *Last Judgement* design on its altar wall.

Christopher Wren, the famed English architect, erected many London churches including St. Bride's. After the Great Fire of London in 1666 he was commissioned to rebuild fifty-one churches, as well as London's wonderful St. Paul's cathedral, which is still his most famous work. Much later, the Spanish architect Antonio Gaudi contributed to the architectural celebration of Christ with his Church of the Holy Family in Barcelona - commenced in 1883.

Christianity's impact on architecture began back in Byzantine times, when churches first took on the Greek cross plan. It continued with the Romanesque style, with the its rounded arches, and through the Gothic period. This featured pointed arches and huge flying buttresses that seem to want to push buildings straight up to heaven. In the Renaissance, major designers like Alberti, Brunelleschi, Bramante and Palladio were all affected by Christian ideas.

In many ways, it was the spread of materialism and scientific rationalism in the twentieth century that brought an effective end to the construction of large, ornate buildings. In the 1930s, a new style took over. It was called Modernism, or Functionalism. As the latter name suggests, it tried to exclude everything that didn't have a clear purpose. Decoration was out, plain was in - and buildings were increasingly erected in honour of a new god, materialism.

As a result, many architects felt that their art had been robbed of much of its soul. It's no accident that the word 'modernism' is also used to describe a theological movement that sprang up at around the same time. It taught that science and philosophy should be given preference over Bible truth. Some modern architects have lamented the lack of spiritual power in the buildings of today. We may need, some have said, a kind of religious revival before we will begin to build again on a really grand and uplifting scale.

Fast Forward...

Of course, the progress and development of art didn't end with the death of the last classical composer, artist or architect. Photography is just one example of a modern art form that's used by men and woman of true genius, to reflect the times in which they live and to help shape those times.

In today's world, the most popular art form might be the movie. Where once people would go to the cathedral to view art, they now pay for a ticket to the cinema. Not all that finds its way onto celluloid can be called art, but the cinema has given us much that is of lasting aesthetic value.

Art-house movies are sometimes acclaimed as fine art by the film buffs and critics. But more populist movies such as *Gone with the Wind, Braveheart* and *Gladiator*, are as valuable for their look and scale as for the epic stories they tell. Orson Welles' masterpiece *Citizen Kane*, voted by many writers the most influential movie of the twentieth century, is certainly a work of some genius.

In our times, we are seeing exciting developments in the fields of movie special effects, virtual reality technology, holographic projection, laser technology and digitised computer and photographic images. All of these technologies offer unprecedented opportunities to the artist who's willing to explore new frontiers.

Writers, illustrators, animators and artists of all kinds are faced with the exciting possibilities offered by the Internet. Some scientists and artists now foresee the day when we will appreciate art not so much through external, physical media, but through direct 'injection' of electrical messages into various parts of our brain.

New forms of artistic expression and fresh works of art will continue to appear, in one form or another, for as long as there is a human soul to appreciate them.

Is God An Art Freak?

Some people think of the Bible's God as someone who basically has an eternal hangover, is grumpy the whole time and just can't wait to step on us like bugs when we look like we're having any fun! In fact, the Old Testament reveals a God who appreciated fine and beautiful things.

What we now call 'the environment', was for centuries known as 'the Creation'. It's a much more picturesque, even artistic term, and it reminds us that you only have to look at a landscape, or an ocean sunset, to see that the One who made it all is something of an artist himself.

Israel's King David, a truly great lyricist and poet, and writer of most of our biblical Psalms, looked at nature and gave us his impressions in verse:

'The heavens declare the glory of God; the skies proclaim the work of his hands. Day after day they pour forth speech; night after night they display knowledge.' (Psalm 19:1-2)

In another of his songs, he sees the wonder and breath-taking scope of God's artistry and responds with this:

'When I consider your heavens, the work of your fingers, the moon and the stars, which you have set in place, what is man that you are mindful of him, the son of man that you care for him?' (Psalm 8:3-4)

Have you ever stood in an art gallery looking at one of those self-portraits? Many times, the artist did the work by holding a mirror to himself. In a way, that's what the Bible says God has done in creating us. He made us in his image or likeness, to reflect something special and unique about his eternal and spiritual nature. No other part of creation bears the same degree of likeness to him.

Imagine a cosmic art gallery is set up in the centre of the universe. It is filled with exhibits from earth, including human beings. Visitors are streaming in from all parts of the galaxy and beyond. How would they respond to what they see? I think they'd be saying something like this: 'The animals are great, and the fauna is fantastic, but the *human being* - that's where you *really* see the Artist expressing himself!'

When you look in the mirror, and consider the incredible complexity of the human body and psyche, you have to admit that God is not just an artist, he is the Ultimate Artist! David said it this way:

'I praise you because I am fearfully and wonderfully made; your works are wonderful, I know that full well.'
(Psalm 139:14)

The Wise Artist

One of Old Testament Israel's most celebrated kings was David's son, Solomon. He was not only an astute man of the world - many of his marriages were motivated by political expediency - he was also gifted in planning and architecture, and in many other fields of science and the arts. One authority writes that, 'No hero of antiquity (with the possible exception of Alexander the Great) is so widely celebrated in folk literature. The Jewish, Arabian and Ethiopian tales about Solomon's intellectual prowess and magical powers are legion.'[5]

Solomon possessed that most rare mix of traits - the scientist's hunger for knowledge and the artist's thirst for beauty. Unlike his father - who was no slouch as a songwriter and lyricist, either - Solomon was a peacetime king and as such he was able to devote his time and energy to things of beauty, to art. The Bible tells us that his talent was a direct gift from God.[6]

Solomon wrote two extensive collections of proverbs.[7] The entire biblical book of Proverbs names him as its chief contributor.[8] In all, he is credited with three thousand proverbs and over one thousand songs.[9] Song of Songs, also known as Song of Solomon and Canticles, is one of the most graphic and beautiful collections of love poems from ancient times. In it, Solomon uses powerful metaphors to describe the love between a groom and his young betrothed. Some have seen it as an allegory that is only meant to point to deeper, spiritual truths, but it's also a celebration of physical beauty and human passion.

The book of Ecclesiastes also suggests that he is its author, though it doesn't mention his name. It is one of history's most moving, honest and artistically woven records of a man's search after truth, and of his ultimate need of God.

Solomon was also an accomplished architect, renowned for the design of his lavish palace and that of his Egyptian-born wife. By far his most significant building, however, was Jerusalem's Temple, which was constructed on the highest point in the city, mount Zion. This is now the site of the Dome of the Rock mosque.

The Temple was the most important building in Israeli society. It housed the Ark of the Covenant, the physical symbol of God's manifest presence with his people. For the Israelites, it was a symbol of their uniqueness among all the nations of the earth. It was also a reminder of God's holiness.

As a piece of architecture, it would have inspired awe in visitors to the Holy City. It's great size meant that it towered over the low-lying dwellings around it. Its golden colour must have made it look like something that had descended straight out of heaven. Its shell was made of huge stones. Each room was panelled with cedar wood and the floor was planked with cypress. The walls and the doors were carved with flowers, palm trees, and cherubim, and then overlaid with gold. No stonework was visible.

On the Temple, Solomon employed famous artists and craftsmen from all points of the compass.[10] These artisans brought with them the major artistic influences of the time. The Temple took seven years to complete,[11] and when the visiting Queen of Sheba saw this building and all of Solomon's other achievements, she was moved to make this remark:

> 'The report I heard in my own country about your achievements and your wisdom is true. But I did not believe what they said until I came and saw with my own eyes. Indeed, not even half the greatness of your wisdom was told me; you have far exceeded the report I heard.' (Chronicles 9:5-6)

Centuries later, the Sistine Chapel was designed using as its basis the exact dimensions of the Solomon's Temple. Its twenty-meter high ceiling became the canvas for some of the art world's most famous frescoes. Solomon would have approved!

Solomon's Temple was an architectural and artistic wonder of the world in its day - for the skill of its construction and for the beauty of its contents. Significantly, God accepted it as the place where he would manifest his special presence in Israel.[12] So, far from being against art, the God of the Old Testament was an avid supporter! The greatest works were created in his honour. In fact, he said that he'd consecrated Solomon's Temple to make his name great![13]

No Graven Images?

What of God's ancient insistence that the people of Israel make no images of him? [14] Was this an attempt to stifle creative expression in their worship and faith, to stop them expressing in artistic form what was most precious to them? No, it was to prevent them from doing either of two things that could spell the very end of their religion, and the nationhood that was built upon it.

Building images for God would, first of all, 'freeze' their concept of him. Once you commit your image of God to stone, you have closed the door on any further revelation. God knew that his people could only know him by progressive revelation - the uncovering of his nature and character to them over time. He did not want them to block that ongoing process by erecting fixed pictures of what he was like.

Secondly, building images would have meant that they were making a god they could manage or control. No matter how much you venerate it, you'll feel much safer with a stone god than with the idea of an infinite, all-knowing and all-seeing God, whom you cannot see or manipulate. Faith is the only mechanism by which we can really experience or personally know God and, as we've seen, faith is about the surrender of control.

God ruled out the building of images of himself because he wanted to protect the purity of the nation's faith, not because he had no taste for sculpture!

God Sees Right Through You!

The God of the Bible is not a Person without taste or an appreciation of the artistic. In fact, it is only because we're made in his image that we have that inner, soul-level taste for higher expression. If Darwin was right, we might well find gorillas writing Shakespeare, or chimps building a Sistine Chapel. The mind boggles!

But there is something else we must know about the God of the Bible. He is not primarily interested in outward appearances, but in the attitudes of our hearts. When God considers a work of art, he does not pay as much attention to the work - fantastic though it might be - as he does to the motivation of heart that produced it.

David was considered a fine looking, athletic man in his time. Perhaps Michelangelo's well-proportioned, highly toned and muscular image of David was not too far from the mark! Yet God specifically told Samuel that the king he would anoint would not be selected because of physical appearance:

'The LORD does not look at the things man looks at. Man looks at the outward appearance, but the LORD looks at the heart.' (1 Samuel 16:7)

Jesus developed this thought many times in his ministry:

'The good man brings good things out of the good stored up in him, and the evil man brings evil things out of the evil stored up in him.' (Matthew 12:35)

Even God's acceptance of the Temple of Solomon was tempered with the condition that the people must remain holy before him.[15] What was most important to God was not the temple, but the separation and purity of heart that first motivated the builders. In God's eyes, a work of art, whilst important and worthwhile in its own right, is temporal and will one day pass away. Many of the greatest works of antiquity, creations that took years or even decades to complete, have now been reduced to dust. But the soul, the essential person-hood of the artist, is eternal. God's greatest concern is its destiny. We concern ourselves only with the art, with what we can see, but God's primary concern is the artist's spiritual condition.

There's an interesting insight into this in the life of Jesus. Just down the road from Nazareth, his hometown, there was a bustling and prosperous city called Sepphoris. It is never mentioned in the gospels, but it was the administrative capital of the Galilee region at the time. Recent archaeological work has shown that it had a very full cultural and artistic life, based on Greek ways and ideas. The residents of this fair city had their own acropolis, a forum, public baths, a royal theatre and a public theatre with four thousand seats.[16] Jesus and his followers could hardly have avoided contact with the influence of this city.

It seems that Jesus was familiar with the arts of his day, though he didn't necessarily look upon them with great favour. For example, he often used the word *hupokrites* to decry the two-faced behaviour of certain classes of religious leaders.[17] We translate the word as 'hypocrite'.

It's interesting that Jesus should choose that word. You see, it was a Greek theatrical word used to describe an actor who played a part in disguise or from behind a mask. Jesus may very well have seen a Greek play. At least he was familiar with the medium and its terminology.

In his use of this word, Jesus may have been, indirectly, showing us a truth about art itself: that art has the potential to provide a very shallow substitute for the thing we really hunger after, a spiritual encounter and relationship with God. If art tries to fill that need it is indeed being hypocritical.

1.   W.E.Vine, *Expository Dictionary of New Testament Words*, (1978).
2.   *Megatrends 2000*, John Naisbitt & Patricia Aburdene, (Pan Books, 1990), pp. 248-9.
3.   Hebrews 11:1
4.   For more on this, see http://www.Christianart.com
5.   *The New Bible Dictionary*, (Inter-Varsity Press, 1978), p. 1202.
6.   1 Kings 4:29
7.   Solomon's proverbs are available to us in Proverbs 10: 1 to 29:27.
8.   Proverbs 1:1
9.   1 Kings 4:32
10.   See 1 Kings 5:10,18 and 7:13-14
11.   See 1 Kings 6:38
12.   1 Kings 9:3
13.   1 Kings 9:7
14.   Exodus 20:3 and Deuteronomy 7:5
15.   1 Kings 9:3-7
16.   Ian Wilson, *Jesus: The Evidence*, (Phoenix Illustrated books, 1998), p. 55.
17.   See Matthew 23

9

Hallelujah!

George Frideric Handel is a good Lutheran, the grandson of a pastor. He's in his fifty-seventh year of life and he's already achieved greatness and notoriety in the field of his particular genius.

Having first impressed people in his native Germany, then in Florence, Venice and Rome, as an organist and harpsichord-player, he has now spent many years carving out his ultimate reputation as a composer. He has been honoured by nobles and employed by kings.

Recently, though, his mind has been plagued with fears that he might end his days in some debtor's prison. Approaching old age, and with his last great success now in the distant past, he has had financial creditors baying for his blood. He needs another hit!

Right now, he's working on something that he hopes will turn a new page in his career. It's an oratorio, written for an upcoming visit to Dublin. He will present it in a series of benefits in aid of prisoners and a local hospital.

The name he's chosen for the work is The Messiah.

He sits with pen in hand; scoring a piece that he will call The Hallelujah Chorus. He doesn't know it yet, but this is destined to become the best known of all his illustrious works, and arguably one of the finest pieces of religious music in history.

As he sits poring over the words, struggling to keep up with the soaring melodies and harmonies that reverberate inside his mind, he begins to weep uncontrollably. There is a presence in his room. He can't explain it: his spirit is suddenly lifted and it's as if he has been given a small taste of the heaven he is writing about.

Later he relates this strange but exhilarating experience to his servant.

'I did think,' he says, 'I did see all heaven before me, and the great God himself!'

Handel's *Messiah* first came to the public's attention at the rehearsal in Dublin on April 8, 1742. The first official presentation was a few days later, on April 13. It was, to put it mildly, a great success.

Handel lived for another seventeen years and led many performances of his immortal work. He conducted the last one only eight days before his death. Charles Burney, the eighteenth century music historian, wrote: '[Handel's *Messiah*] fed the hungry, clothed the naked, and fostered the orphan.'

Art Provokes

God is not against art. In fact, it might be said that at different times art has set itself up against him!

When artists turn, for example, to graphic portrayals of violence or to pornography, they are dishonouring the One who gave them their creative gifts. They are celebrating things that work against his honour, and pull down the dignity of the human spirit. But in the right hands, art can elevate the human soul, lifting us closer to God.

Now, you may be thinking, 'I'm no artist. I haven't painted anything since kindergarten - except for my house.' That may be true, but you *are* creative. God has placed within each of us a capacity to imagine and to bring into reality what is only now a dream - in other words, to create. You may not be an artist with paint and canvas but you may, for example, be an artist with money - someone who can create wealth. Or, you may be creative with words - someone who sells an idea with ease, because you express concepts with clarity and passion. Whatever your creative bent, the question for this chapter is this: how can you use your creativity for God's glory?

And, for those who are musicians, writers, choreographers, photographers, architects, graphic designers, and so on, how can you use your particular art form to make God famous?

Art has an uncanny knack of challenging our values and traditional concepts. It unsettles our ideas of how things should be seen and done. It can provoke us into looking for something higher and better than we presently see. Men like Amos, Jeremiah, Isaiah and Hosea were forever challenging the status quo.[1] The prophet's work was preparing the way of the Lord, and, 'making the road straight for him.'[2]

In the New Testament, we see the prophetic role taken up by John the Baptist. In perhaps true artistic tradition, he took to wearing unusual clothes made of camel's hair (ouch!) and eating wild honey. His message was just as prickly:

'Change your hearts and lives because the kingdom of heaven is near.' (Matthew 3:2-3)

In every case, the prophetic voice did two things: it called people back to right relationship with God, and it called them into proper harmony with their fellow man. It was both a God-ward and a man-ward message.

Throughout history, many prophetic people have employed artistic media to confront and challenge. Martin Luther wrote many hymns, some of them drawing on the pub tunes of his day. His followers presented his teaching in picture form using lithographs and woodblocks.

In a later age, John and Charles Wesley used music, literature and poetry to spread their message. The founders of the Salvation Army, William and Catherine Booth really understood the power of poster art - long before it became the popular medium it is today. Their posters, plastered all over London, told of 'Holy War!' and other such stirring themes. They used art to get people thinking about the state of their souls and their society.

In our own day, art produced by Christians should do more than soothe. Art's role is to comfort the afflicted and afflict the comfortable. So much Christian music in recent days has been built around 'me' and 'my needs', when it should prophetically point us toward our relationships with God and other people.

Being prophetic is risky business; it may come at the price of popularity or easy acceptance. You cannot, after all, be prophetically correct and *politically correct* at the same time! History shows us, though, that the people we come to admire most are often those who have challenged us most. When our art does nothing more than echo the individualistic, egocentric cries of the age, people shut off to it. Because it has nothing new to say to them, it does not command their attention, or their respect.

Art Models

One of the most fascinating things about many of the Old Testament prophets was the graphic - even eccentric - methods they used to get their message across. They used powerful object lessons to illustrate a truth. Sometimes the lesson was wrapped up in their very lives. God knows it's true: a picture *does* paint a thousand words.

Think about it: what's the basis of most advertising? It's the power of pictures, the power of modelling. The desire to see a truth not just told, but modelled, is in the human wiring. It lies at the deepest level of our psyche, because that's the way God is. God's favourite means of communication is incarnation. He wraps the message, the truth, in human form - or in pictures we can understand.

To Abraham, God said, 'Look at the stars - that's how many children you will have!' To Moses, he spoke from a bush that burned and yet was not consumed. That bush wasn't just God using special effects. It was an 'incarnation', a model of what Moses was to become. He would be a man so burning with a vision from a higher place, that people would take their shoes off for fear of God.

Jesus was a Prophet - the greatest of them all, for he was God's Son. He cried out against ungodliness and human injustice and emphasised a changed life. His stories were totally captivating - they still are. That's because they conjure in our mind scenes to which we can easily relate. They're stories about runaway kids, greedy businessmen, lost property, making investments, working the land, and much more.

Jesus often used hyperbole to make a vivid point. This is a form of humour - comedy, if you like - which relies on exaggerating something to the point of the ridiculous. It gets people thinking. He told some nit-picking religious leaders that they reminded him of someone who swallows a camel, but chokes on a mosquito.[3] Another time, he told them that they shouldn't try to pick a splinter out of a friend's eye until they've first removed the huge pylon from their own.[4]

There's something very cartoon-like about those pictures. I wonder what Jesus might have done with animation!

In a way, art can model a truth for us, putting a message or concept in a form with which we can readily identify.

Art Captivates

The best art provokes a response, both mentally and emotionally. If it can impact us in those two areas it can change our behaviour. There are two dangers we should avoid if we are to make God famous through our creative abilities.

The first is art that's all heart. This is creative expression that's loaded with emotion, but provides no stimulus for people to think. We're living in what author John Smith once called an 'analgesic society', where people are looking for ways to kill their pain. The pills we use are not always literal drugs - sex and entertainment can also provide an easy escape. People want to feel good, but they don't necessarily want to think or plan ahead. In the face of this, part of the role of the Christian artist is to challenge people to face where their lives are right now, and where they may be headed.

Our creativity must avoid worn-out cliches, whether in visual form or in language. They represent laziness on our part and do nothing to arouse spiritual hunger. When Jesus told his audience parables, he wasn't giving them bedtime stories to send them off to the land of Nod. He was challenging them to wake up, to think and interact with his message.

Now there is, of course, a fundamental difference between art and, say, most preaching. Preaching is most often more polemic than art: it calls a spade a spade, straight out. It speaks in black and white, direct terms. Preaching is usually at its best when it is direct and black and white (though, of course, if more preachers were inventive in their work, more people would listen!). Art, on the other hand, ceases to be art when it becomes too 'easy to read'. It needs to challenge us to arrive at a conclusion for ourselves.

Christian art - or art by Christians - may not give us all the answers in one line, but it must challenge us to move closer to truth for ourselves. It shouldn't just leave us hanging out in the breeze, without a clue as to where to go from here.

Jesus told stories that not only hooked people emotionally; they provoked people to think. Having finished a story, he would leave his hearers to ponder the meaning behind it. He told his disciples that people who were really *trying* to understand - who were really *hungry* for God's truth - would get the message without too much trouble. The truth, he said, would be clear to anyone who had 'ears to hear.'[5]

By making his audience interact with the teaching in this way, Jesus was making sure they would not forget what he had said. They would really 'own' what he was saying and start applying it to their lives.

In a way, his teaching was very black and white - there was no compromise between truth and error, or right and wrong. Yet Jesus did not insult the intelligence of his hearers. He made people face truth for themselves.

The second thing we must avoid is expression that has no *emotional* pull. So many people in our generation have a very dispassionate view of God. Their attitude toward Christianity is one of outright disinterest, mainly because they've never felt that God is particularly interested in them!

The ancient Greeks taught that three factors govern all communication: *ethos*, the credibility of the communicator; *logos*, the intellectual content of the message; *pathos*, the passion of the communicator and the emotions engendered in the audience. How does the most successful advertising work? It often concentrates more on pathos than on anything else; it aims to encourage an emotional response, because people 'think' with their hearts as well as with their heads.

People are often moved into action by their feelings, rather than their thoughts. Our art should reflect a real empathy for people's feelings, and a real desire to point them to someone who can really help.

The God Of Passion

Contrary to popular opinion, the God of the Bible is not a bland Person who is devoid of feelings. Of course, it would be wrong to say that God is emotional in the same way that we are. For one thing, the degenerative effects of sin daily influence our emotions. We are, at times, driven along by powerful feelings over which we feel we have very little control. God's actions, on the other hand, are never impacted by flights of fancy, or spur-of-the-moment whims, or seemingly uncontrollable temper tantrums. God is not emotional in the same way that we are. Yet, our emotions are a part of God's creation and, in their unfallen state, they represented a part of God's own nature.

Even a cursory reading of the Bible reveals a God who is a very passionate Person! The Old Testament is replete with adjectives for God that reflect the strength of his feelings. For example, God is described as being filled with burning anger toward his enemies and the enemies of his people;[6] protectively jealous for his people;[7] and filled with zeal for those whom he's chosen.[8] The prophet Zephaniah brought this word to Israel:

> 'The LORD your God is with you, he is mighty to save. He will take great delight in you, he will quiet you with his love, he will rejoice over you with singing.' (Zephaniah 3:17)

In the Hebrew original, the language is much more potent. The latter part of the verse says something more like this: 'God wants to spin around you under the influence of violent emotion.' Far from being undemonstrative or emotionless, this God is filled with ardour for his people!

Old Testament men and women who earned God's approval were also passionate. David, for example, was described as a man after God's own heart.[9] He had an attitude, a disposition toward God and other people, that God could bless. What, in particular, did God like about David? Perhaps the one defining characteristic of David's personality was his passion, his ability to turn strong feelings into bold action.

David was, for example, passionate in war. As a teenager, he faced a nine-foot-six-inch tall NBA-wannabe named Goliath. This giant, the champion of the Philistines, had thrown down a challenge to the whole Israeli army. 'Send me a man to fight,' he demanded. 'If you've got one!' The brave men of Israel did what many of us would have done: they looked at the odds against them and opted not to throw the dice. But what was David's response?

*'Who is this uncircumcised Philistine that he should
defy the armies of the living God?' (1 Sam 17:26)*

Big words for a sixteen-year-old kid! At the end of
the day, though, it was the red-hot enthusiasm of this
untrained youngster that brought down a colossus and
led Israel to a massive victory.

David was passionate in worship, too. When the ark
of God's covenant was being returned to its rightful home
in Jerusalem, David just couldn't resist throwing off his
kingly robes for a day, to dance before the Lord.[10] In doing
this, David was effectively playing the role of court jester. In a royal procession, the jester's role was to make
people laugh and feel good about the arrival of their
monarch. David was deliberately humbling himself before
the King of all kings, out of his fiery love for God.

Wouldn't it be refreshing today to find more gifted
artists who don't mind copping some ridicule for the way
they live and worship - who don't mind being
misunderstood - because their greatest passion is
expressed for God's benefit, and not just for the pleasure
of the audience?

David was also passionate in love. This was, of
course, something that landed him in hot water! He fell
head-over-heels in love with another man's wife and,
having made Bathsheba pregnant, he manipulated
events to have her husband killed in battle.[11]

Yet, when confronted by the prophet Nathan with
the enormity of his sins, David responded once more
with passion, this time in a heart-wrenching cry of
repentance. Nobody who reads Psalm 51 with an ounce
of humanity can fail to empathise with the sheer agony
of soul David felt at the time, or with his desperate need
of redemption.

Is God passionate? Look at the life of Jesus. Here
was a man who knew how to weep. Here was a man who
knew how to laugh. Here was a man who was so unlike
the stuck-up religious leaders of his day that sinners
were drawn to him like a magnet. Here was a man who

knew more about what the French call 'the joy of life' than any person before or since. Knowing that he was born to die, he still packed more *living* into each day than anyone else has ever done! And he defined his mission on earth as one of giving others his kind of life - life to the max, a passionate life.[12]

In the end, art that does not *move* us, that does not fire some passion deep within our souls, can never point us to God.

Art Sets the Imagination on Fire!

Faith is the ability to see the unseen, to consider as real what is, as yet, unreal. The Amplified Version of the Bible tells us that faith is, 'perceiving as real fact what is not revealed to the senses.'[13] If that's what faith is, then it ought to be a great help to an artist! After all, an artist is, 'A person who displays in his work qualities required in art, such as sensibility and imagination.'[14]

Faith works from the field of the image into the field of reality. As we develop our spiritual life of faith, we learn to tune and strengthen our God-given power to imagine, and therefore to create. What's more, our creative imagination becomes coloured with the images that are most honouring to God. Our hearts are fired with his passion for other people and for his world.

When you fall in love with someone, you learn to appreciate things they appreciate. Your heart is keen to like what they like and to see the world as they do. The more your love grows, the more your senses start to take in the world as they see, hear and feel it. When creative people begin a daily relationship with God through Christ, they find that they begin to see things around them with a new clarity and with a greater appreciation, as gifts from God. Their senses become attuned to like what he likes, to see what he sees. Their art begins to take on a new level of perception, insight and expression.

Christians need to reclaim the ground we have lost when it comes to influence through the arts. It was God who gave us our artistic tastes and creative drives. We can honour the Giver by releasing and revealing the gift. If we are prepared to use creative expression to celebrate and give thanks to God. If we are hungry to point people toward God and toward each other. If we are sharpening the eye of faith, through worship, prayer and Bible study, we'll see God increase our creativity and bless us with an exhilarating - yes, and sobering - vision of the world as he sees it. Releasing our creativity in line with that vision will truly *make God famous*!

1. See Hosea 4:1-3 and 6:1; Amos 4:1 and 5:4,6,14
2. Isaiah 40:3
3. Matthew 23:24
4. Luke 6:41
5. Mark 4:9
6. Exodus 15:7 and Ezekiel 38:18
7. Malachi 3:17
8. Isaiah 26:11
9. 1 Samuel 13:14
10. 2 Samuel 6:14
11. 2 Samuel 11:3-5 and 14-17
12. John 10:10
13. Hebrews 11:1, *The Amplified Bible.*
14. *Collins Concise Dictionary*

About the Author

Mal Fletcher is a respected Christian leader, TV presenter and internationally acclaimed speaker. In his unique and challenging style, he is bringing the Christian message to secular cultures via the media and large outreach events around the world.

Originally from Australia, Mal is now well known in many nations as a pioneer leader and for his unique ability to communicate Christian truth in a thought-provoking, insightful and often humourous way that relates to secular and Christian audiences alike.

His TV programs, *EDGES with Mal Fletcher*, are seen in over 60 countries, and he leads the *Generals* and *EYE* leadership networks across Europe. These bring together two generations of key apostolic Christian leaders in Europe for strategic planning and prayer.

Mal is the founder of *Next W@ve International*, a mission to the contemporary cultures of Europe. Through this rapidly expanding mission, he and his team are not only reaching the unchurched via city-wide events, the Internet, media and more; they are also equipping church and business leaders in the skills of contemporary leadership. The *Leadership Now* Master Classes on leadership attract leaders from many nations.

Mal was raised in a Christian home, and studied architecture in his home city of Melbourne before feeling a call to full time ministry in the early 1980s. Throughout the 80s and early 90s, he was the key person God used to motivate and facilitate the formation of *Youth Alive Australia*, a youth movement committed to the local church. He was its first National Director. This exciting movement grew from just 300 young people to over 60,000 in 10 years, as the Spirit of God moved among that nation's youth and churches. It continues to grow and its model is now influencing many nations for Jesus.

He also pioneered a church in one of his country's leading new age and occult areas. His books on culture and leadership issues are now available in several languages.

Today, as well as heading up the mission to Europe, Mal travels the world extensively teaching and preaching at leadership conferences and events. He has been married to Davina for twenty-one years and they have three children. They live in Copenhagen Denmark.

Information on Mal's personal appearances, plus photo's, articles and the Next W@ve movie can be found at: www.nextwaveinternational.com

So, You've Enjoyed Reading This Book?

Order Your Copy of

Book 2

In this MAKING GOD FAMOUS (MGF) Series by MAL FLETCHER

Order ONLINE from the Making God Famous website

at: **www.godfamous.com**

Also ONLINE:

- Information about other books in the MGF series, and coming titles.
- Other books, teaching tapes, CD-ROMs, and videos by Mal Fletcher.
- News on Live Appearances by Mal Fletcher - around the world.
- Information about the mission of Next W@ve International in Europe and beyond.

Other books by Mal Fletcher:

Youth: The Endangered Species
Get Real!
Burning Questions
The Joseph Chronicles

YOU

CAN HELP MAL FLETCHER AND HIS TEAM

Make a Permanent Impact on Europe!

According to respected Christian leaders like C. Peter Wagner, Western Europe now represents perhaps the darkest region on earth, in spiritual terms.

Every day, 30,000 people come to Christ in Latin America.
Every day, 25,000 come to Christ in China.
Every day, 15,000 come to Christ in Africa.

Every day, thousands of people leave the church in Europe!
NEXT W@VE INTERNATIONAL
is helping to reshape Europe's spiritual future!

--✂------

YES! I want to help Mal and his international team by investing in this rapidly growing mission across Europe:

Name: _____

Address: _____

E-mail: _____ Phone: _____

Please debit my:

Visa ☐   Master Card ☐   American Express ☐

Card Number ☐☐☐☐-☐☐☐☐-☐☐☐☐-☐☐☐☐

Amount (Please include your currency): _____

This is a:
☐ Monthly Pledge   ☐ One-Time Gift

Name on Card: _____

Expiry Date: ___ / ___   Signature: _____

Mail/Fax to:

EUROPE/BRITAIN/USA/CANADA:

Next W@ve International, Drejervej 11-21, 2400-Copenhagen NV, Denmark, Fax: +45-3531-0096

AUSTRALIA/NEW ZEALAND/ASIA: Next W@ve International, P.O. Box 93, O'Halloran Hill, S.A., 5158, Australia, Fax: +61-8-83228101

(You can also make a donation online at: www.nextwaveinternational.com)